Non-Fungible Tokens

Introduction To a New Era
How to Create, Buy, and Sell NFTs
An Easy Guide to Crypto Arts

Steve Limes

© Copyright (Non-Fungible Tokens) By Steve Limes

All rights reserved.

Copyrights Notice

No part of this book may be reproduced in any form or by any electronic or mechanical means, including information storage and retrieval systems, without written permission from the author.

Recording of this publication is strictly prohibited, and any storage of this document is not allowed unless with written permission from the publisher.

All rights reserved. Respective authors own all copyrights not held by the publisher.

Pictures inside this book are of the respective owners, granted to the Author in a Royalty-Free license.

All trademarks, service marks, product names and the characteristics of any names mentioned in this book are considered the property of their respective owners and are used only for reference. No endorsement is implied when we use one of these terms.

Limited Liability - Disclaimer

Please note that the content of this book is based on personal experience and various information sources, and it is only for personal use.

Please note the information contained within this document is for educational and entertainment purposes only, and no warranties of any kind are declared or implied.

Readers acknowledge that the author is not engaging in the rendering of legal, financial, or professional advice. Please consult a licensed professional before attempting any techniques outlined in this book.

Nothing in this book is intended to replace common sense or legal accounting, or professional advice and is meant only to inform.

Your particular circumstances may not be suited to the example illustrated in this book; in fact, they likely will not be.

You should use the information in this book at your own risk. The reader is responsible for his or her actions.

The information provided herein is stated to be truthful and consistent, in that any liability, in terms of inattention or otherwise, by any usage or abuse of any policies, processes or directions contained within is the solitary and utter responsibility of the recipient reader.

By reading this book, the reader agrees that under no circumstances is the author responsible for any losses, direct or indirect, which are incurred as a result of the use of the information contained within this document, including, but not limited to, errors, omissions or inaccuracies.

Table of Contents

Non-Fungible Tokens	1
Copyrights Notice	2
Limited Liability - Disclaimer	3
Table of Contents	4
Introduction	6
Chapter 1. Non-fungible Token	8
Characteristics of NFTs	13
Hype for art	17
ASSET FOR COLLECTIBLES	20
Chapter 2. History of	23
Non-fungible Tokens	23
Problems or Controversies	27
Chapter 3. Cases of use of	29
Non-fungible Token	29
What are ERC-721 tokens?	31
Important Information	31
What we can convert to NFT	34
Some Famous NFT Projects	35
Top NFT Projects	37
Latest Sells of NFTs	38
Chapter 4. Security and	46
Non-fungible Token	46
NFT Risks and Scams & How to Avoid them	51
NFT Major Trading Risks	52

Wash Trades	54
NFT Scams You Must Avoid	55
Chapter 5. Platform to Sell NFT and its Requirement	62
Chapter 6. How to Create NFTs	68
What can NFTs do?	73
They sold millions of dollars, with some rare artefacts bringing hundreds of thousands.	74
Detailed steps on how to create NFT art	75
Divided Opinion on NFTs	78
Celebrities and NFTs	79
Growing	80
Next Move?	81
Selling an NFT	81
Creating a collection	82
Projects build a strong foundation under the DEFI and NFTS marriage	84
Chapter 7. NFT Lending & Borrowing	93
Chapter 8. Other Options to Get Exposures to NFTs	103
Chapter 9. FAQs Related to NFTs	108
Chapter 10. Future of Non Fungible Tokens	117
Conclusion	121

Introduction

The concept of trustless digital scarcity was developed when Bitcoin was created. However, the expensive digital copies proved to be a hurdle in the way of using this technology over a broader spectrum.

It is now possible to create programmable digital scarcity because of the arrival of blockchain technology. Previously there was a gap between the real and digital worlds, which has now been covered using this technology. The first sort of digital asset that can be played is non-fungible tokens (NFTs). This could act as a catalyst for increasing the scarcity of digital products.

Because ERC-721 tokens are not interchangeable, they can be used to represent one-of-a-kind assets and ideas. In other words, this model can accurately represent real things such as real estate, artwork and antiques.

The collectibles market is now over $450 billion and has remained relatively unchanged since the internet's inception. Authentication issues, fraud and monetary constraints are all too typical in the industry. In a trustless age where online transactions are considered as risky business, blockchain technology is building a new era of risk-free transactions.

Real-world assets can be tokenized using NFTs, which are both trustworthy and untrustworthy.

The NFT market was built around Ethereum for the most part. However, people have become more interested in EOS due to the increased activities. As a result, it's no surprise that non-fungible tokens (NFTs) are popping up on new blockchains due to investment supporting development.

NFTs (non-fungible tokens) are digital assets with unique properties. The object's digital representation might be generated using these specific properties. Focus areas could be used to symbolize physical products in the actual world. Instead of being dependent on a centralized authority, a decentralized or a distributed ledger that is owned by a community can be used for exchanges between each other.

NFT is a digital asset that owns the digitized crypto based tokens. We'll go through the many characteristics of NFTs and how they relate to other asset classes.

This book will cover the following topics:

Polyhedral tessellations

As previously said, NFTs come in a range of forms and sizes.

Tokens of various types (fungible and non-fungible) (NFTs).

An explanation of NFTs and digital assets. Concerns about legal and ethical issues surrounding the development of NFTs.

Other concerns about NFTs include relating to photographers, musicians and videographers.

We'll also address several of the most common inquiries concerning NFTs and related applications.

We will also learn about creating NFTs using Ether.

Chapter 1. Non-fungible Token

NFTs are digital crypto based assets available in virtual environments in the form of digital art or virtual real estate. NFTs are as one-of-a-kind as actual works of art. To detect the difference between a replica and an original, blockchain technology is employed to recognize their validity.

This qualified it as a data carrier that acts as a digital representation of a tangible item. It represents real estate, artwork, collectibles and other physical goods. This kind of digital asset has been heralded as the global economy's next stage.

They make it possible to safely store and transfer a significant investment on the chain. On this chain, any publisher can be traced with his artwork. This can be utilized to avoid the fraud and manipulation that plagues today's markets.

Cryptokitties and Cryptopunks are two of the most well-known varieties of NFTs.

NFTs are a one-of-a-kind digital asset. To be precise, they are the first significant digital asset type to be tokenized on the blockchain.

We call these non-fungible assets tokens since they don't have the fungible qualities of ordinary digital assets. Non-fungible tickets

(NFTs) cannot be changed or replicated without altering the tangible asset value they reflect.

NFT uses this functionality to provide buyers with digital item ownership certificates and to preserve the value of their prospective transactions. According to a CoinDesk study, artists can digitally market their artwork to a global audience, increasing income for one-piece works and royalty schemes. NFTs are a significant improvement over previous forms of tokens.

Gamers can also buy and sell in-game property and items to make money. The ERC-1155 and ERC-721 Ethereum standards are used to create most NFT tokens.

According to Cryptokitties, Digital collectibles can be used as a proof of concept by NFTs. While this is a tiny application, it indicates that NFTs are a novel and unique technology. They've laid the groundwork for taking scarcity and digital ownership to entirely new heights.

The interest has been shifted due to increased activity on EOS. With investment fueling blockchain expansion, it's no wonder that NFTs are beginning to surface on new blockchains.

NFTs are still very young, with only a few essential applications to date. It is also true that future applications are going to benefit from NFTs a lot.

With the rise of digital asset exchanges, a new sort of liquidity that was previously unavailable will be available. Currently, if we have a look at the NFT market, we will find similar conditions to that of Bitcoin's conditions in the early days.

The way NFTs are defined and classified still has a lot of flaws. Moreover, we have no universally accepted standard for their generation and storage.

Although the NFT market is still in its early stages, it has already demonstrated its utility in specialized needs. This technology will take some time to be deployed in various applications, but that does not rule out its potential in the future.

These possible applications will necessitate a solution to the NFT interoperability issue.

Nobody owns anything in the real world. Only persons who are registered as its owner on a blockchain can possess the real-world sets that NFTs represent. Only if the value of NFTs can be transferred on the blockchain can they be effectively owned and controlled.

The majority of people already have knowledge related to digital assets like gaming assets, digital tickets, songs, and more such items. Because NFTs have had success in various areas thus far, there will only be greater adoption in the future.

The demand for NFTs will rise as the public becomes more acclimated to using bitcoin exchange platforms. Many people believe that blockchain technology will disrupt many industries. However, online gaming is the market where this could happen first. If NFTs can be used on the blockchain, they will bring up many opportunities for the gaming sector.

NFTs have already begun to be used in video games. NFTs are already being used by many developers for gaming assets. They've released these NFTs for gamers to utilize in their favorite games. The fact that these assets are maintained on the blockchain adds to their general acceptance.

NFTs aren't just for inside games, either. We can use NFTs for several reasons outside of the gaming sector. NFTs can be used as collectibles or for in-app purchases.

What is NFTs

Cryptocurrency functions similarly to physical money in that it is fungible. We can say it can be used to purchase and sell items, as well as to convert one currency into another. One bitcoin, for example, will always be worth the same as another bitcoin. The Ether is in the same boat. Because of its fungibility, cryptocurrency is regarded as a secure transaction medium in the digital economy.

NFTs alter the crypto landscape by making each token unique and irreplaceable, and non-fungible, which means that one token may be valued more than the others.

To distinguish digital asset representations from other tokens, they are equated with digital passports due to their distinct and nontransferable ID. There is growth potential. To put it another way, two NFTs can "breed" to create a third, distinct NFFT.

NFTs, like Bitcoin, provide extensive ownership information to make the process of verification and token exchange between holders simpler. The NFT allows asset owners to add metadata or attributes relating to their assets. Fairtrade beans, for example, can be considered a token.

Artists can also sign their digital artworks with their metadata signature.

The same individual administering the ERC-20 Intelligent Contract utilized the ERC-721 standard to create NFTs. The ERC-721 standard has explained the specifications for gaming token trading. The ERC-1155 standard is characterized as lowering transaction and storage costs in a single contract as needed for non-fungible tokens and batches in various non-fungible tokens.

The release of Cryptokitties, the most notable episode in NFT history, occurred in November 2017. Cryptokitties are depicted as digital cats with a unique Ethereum Blockchain ID.

Each kitten is fantastic, and it is traded in Ether. They reproduce with one another and produce new offspring with characteristics and assessments that differ from their parents. Cryptokitties instantly attracted a lot of users that spent almost 20 million dollars in Ether exchange and purchase.

Some fans go to great lengths in their efforts, even going as far as to pay $100,000.

Although Cryptokitties is not well recognized, it has enormous commercial implications. NFTs, for example, have been employed in both real estate and personal transactions. Allowing several sorts of tokens in agreements boosts trust in such tickets, whether they're used for property investment or single operations.

Fungibility in NFTs

If any asset has the ability to be exchanged for something similar without having any effect on its value, this is what we call fungibility. The features like divisibility and the value of an asset are also defined by fungibility.

When two $ 10 bills are compared, their worth is the same. Instead of returning a $ 10 account, for example, you might return it in the form of another sort of currency with the same value.

One BTC is valued roughly the same as the other in the realm of digital money. On the other hand, tokens that aren't fungible aren't fungible. In this instance, the NFT token will have a different value than equivalent tokens. Each token has its distinct qualities and real-world assets, such as precious stones, artworks and the collector's luxury goods.

Fungible and non-fungible

Fungible tokens are those whose value does not change when they are exchanged. As explained before, the owner of Bitcoin and the history of transactions have no effect on the value of Bitcoin. This is why it's called a fungible token.

Non-fungible tokens, on the other hand, are separate from one another and cannot be traded in any other form. As previously described with the bitcoin, a non-fungible token, on the other hand, is a one-of-a-kind trade card.

Characteristics of NFTs

Rarity

The NFT's worth is determined by its rarity. As a result, NFT developers can create the required number of tokens, and to improve their value, they occasionally limit the development of these tokens.

NFTs are inseparable from each other. You may buy a whole piece of digital art or not purchase any art at all.

The most important feature is that it is unique. They create a permanent information tab in which they identify themselves as one-of-a-kind. These characteristics are regarded as an originality certificate by them.

Creating your own NFT artwork, whether as a GIF or a picture, is a straightforward process that requires little or no cryptocurrency understanding. NFT may be used to make both physical collectibles and digital card stacks.

It is possible to shift a picture developed on one chain to another since the blockchain generates the art. Some software like photoshop etc. can be used to create NFTs. To make your image usable by Etheremon or similar games, you'll need to convert it to an ASCII art file. Some digital art tools, such as Gimp, allow you to encode the file in base64 or an image format that Etheremon understands.

You can understand the concept of creating NFT by converting your digital art into a visual format. You may use Gimp to convert your digital work to the correct file type. At last, you will need to upload your art on the blockchain.

How much making an NFT cost?

Fortunately, we have a lot of free programs available for creating NFTs! Etheremon, CryptoKitties and CryptoPunks are just a few available tools. Tools like Gimp can also be used to create digital art.

One of the most critical tasks is account creation for your NFT. Like all other digital assets, registering your NFT on a blockchain using wallets like MyEtherWallet or MetaMask is crucial.

To design and administer NFTs on the Ethereum blockchain, developers can use open-source tools like the ERC-721. Developers can also use various third-party programs to construct and manage NFTs. Ethers.JS is an example of one of these. NFTs aren't just for games; they have a lot of other uses as well. NFTs have a variety of applications outside of games, including:

• Art Industry: Artists can sell their digital work here.

• Real Estate: NFT may be used to easily transact digital real estate and 3D goods such as furniture.

• Musicians: They can sell their content's rights or short videos.

NFTs can be employed in so many ways in games, making them so intriguing for game makers. The size and complexity of NFTs on games are two of the limits that creators encounter with them.

NFTs are beginning to look like a viable solution as more developers explore these possibilities.

An NFT is a relatively new gaming technology that allows for compelling and flexible virtual products and experiences. Ethereum smart contracts can be used to exchange a virtual item without worrying about physical deals. These contracts are valuable in a variety of industries, including games.

Option of leasing listing is also available for those sellers who do not have much time and money to spend on attracting buyers to their property. It is feasible to create a contract that lays out how the virtual asset will be used and what will occur if the civil action arises. The contract may also include instructions describing how items in the virtual world must behave following the design criteria.

In comparison to digital currencies, NFTs are more closely considered digital assets. The asset must be unique to be exchanged between two users. These tokens are neither interchangeable nor divisible since their value fluctuates due to supply and demand fluctuations.

Where to use NFTs?

The NFTs have a lot of uses. Here are a few examples:

NFTs are extremely rare and one-of-a-kind. You can build operable real-world assets on the blockchain by combining NFTs and digital IDs. Because traditional digital products lack ownership and scarcity, they cannot be classified as real-world assets. Because smart contracts are used to implement NFTs, they can have fungible digital identities, allowing them to operate as real-world assets.

Smart contracts can be made more accessible with NFTs. This means they can handle escrows, in-game purchases, and other things as well. They can do these duties and adding a new degree of complexity. The rise in complexity has several good consequences for all parties involved.

Another application is swapping digital assets for physical ones utilizing NFTs as the transaction medium. Although this concept is more common in the gaming sector as compared to other sectors, the concept of exchanging digital products for real-world items is not limited to that.

NFTs are mainly utilized in the gaming industry to purchase digital objects. Because they can access their NFTs from anywhere, they have more freedom and control over their assets.

These virtual assets are significantly secure and more noticeable than ordinary digital products because they are housed on the blockchain. This means that interacting with NFTs carries a lower risk of fraud and fraud. If players wish to trade their digital items outside of the game, they can easily do so utilizing NFTs as the medium of transaction.

A user's profile includes a collection of digital assets in addition to their in-game credentials and scores. This gives them complete control over these assets while also allowing them to be used most efficiently feasible. CryptoKitties, for example, is a good illustration of this. CryptoKitties is an online collectibles game that focuses on digital items. It enables users to buy and collect kittens, which can then be traded and sold the same way as other digital commodities may.

When a player buys CryptoKitties, they acquire blockchain-based virtual assets. These virtual items are one-of-a-kind and can only be handled by the player. This eliminates the possibility of being conned or losing access to them.

The Art Market's Future in the Blockchain Space

If the dreamers have their way, NFTs, blockchain and ethers will be distinguished in the future. If the doubters get their way, subsequent hype will drive up the price of art in comparison to a poor work of art.

A person from US named Mike Winkelmann has not missed a single day for 13 years when he has not released a piece in the market. Justin Bieber wore his artwork on stage, and Louis Vuitton made garments with it. He is a graphic designer as well and a father. And because he's done it, it's evident that art is something he's done before. And painting has undoubtedly been something he has done in the past since it is something he has chosen for himself. On his website, he says, "He dabbles in various artistic pursuits. Some of it is decent, but most of it is awful (so, bear with him as he strives to make it less garbage every day)."

He set up an auction on Nifty Gateway, earning over $ 3.5 million for around 20 artworks.

Hype for art

The headline of "Esquire" a few days ago was Beeple Mania's story of making Millions selling digital arts. In addition, Beeple Mania is surrounded by cat crazy. The New York Times' headline on Monday reads, "Why an Animation Flying Cat with a Pop-Tart Body selling for almost $ 600,000."

Everything is available in the art market. The cost of each piece of art is relatively high, and the material is constantly changing. Things don't seem to be like they've always been at present because digital art that formerly had no marketplace is suddenly being sold. It's already gone like hotcakes on the markets, even though practically everyone in the art world has noticed. Nifty

Gateway, Foundation, Rare, SuperRare, MakersPlace, Zora and KnownOrigin are the most well-known art marketplaces.

All of this needs a lot of discussion. So, what's the big deal here? First question is, why do people of Clubhouse buy digital art? What do you expect to do with it? In all of this, what role do NFTs play? What are NFTs, exactly? A social network known as Clubhouse has been working to make people aware of NFTs and its future.

I first heard the sentence "NFTs and the Future of the Art" while sitting in the room, and I still hear it now and then. Some users frequently discuss the downsides of crypto wallets, sudden drops in cryptocurrencies, and tokens like ETH, BTC, Nifty, and SuperRare.

Those that know their way around always hunt for new ideas and knowledge with the passage of time. If you don't know anything about NFT, you'll feel ashamed and upset, and you'll leave the room right away. Let's say a digital artist sells a piece of art for $1.4 million in five minutes. If you aren't familiar with marketplace drop culture, you won't comprehend specific quantities.

Key functions

NFTs are more advanced versions of basic encryption. The modern financial system includes complex trading and lending mechanisms for various assets, ranging from real estate to loans and artworks. NFTs are upgrading this infrastructure to allow for the representation of digital, physical assets. To ensure that the concept of digital, physical asset separation isn't novel and that it doesn't necessitate separate identification. Although combined with the advantages of scalability-resistant intelligent contracts, blockchain might become a powerful force for change.

Perhaps the market's efficiency benefits NFT directly. Converting actual benefits into digital works may eliminate intermediaries and simplify the process.

NFTs in block diagrams depicting accurate or digital drawings eliminate the need for agencies and allow artists to communicate directly with their audiences. They may also improve their business operations. For example, the NFT of a bottle of wine will make it easier to connect and manage each supply chain member's source, manufacture, and sales. A customer solution has been developed by Ernst & Young.

Non-fungible tokens are also fantastic for keeping track of identities. Just imagine if we could use digital art or NFTs as unique identities instead of passports for entering and leaving countries. NFT might be used for identity management in the digital world to broaden this application.

By separating them into varying amounts of tangible assets, such as property, NFT may offer a new investing concept. It is more convenient to shuffle virtual real estate assets as compared to physical assets. This tokenization ethic does not need to be limited to real estate. It's simple to extend to other resources, such as photos.

Consequently, the art is not limited to only one owner. A digital equivalent may exist, and each owner is responsible for a diagram section. These contracts have the potential to increase their value and earnings. NFTs can create new types of investing and markets.

Benefit of NFT

Non-fungible tokens provide the digital world with a new dimension. The following are some of the major advantages of NFTs: NFTs are transferable, unlike exchangeable tokens on commercial exchanges. A particular of NFT is where it is bought and sold. However, its worth is determined by itself.

They exist: an NFT coin represents the technological power of blockchain. Consequently, you may be confident that your NFT is authentic, as forgeries are nearly hard to create with such a decentralized and unchangeable master book.

They are the owners of the property. It also means that in a decentralized environment, the owner of digital art cannot change his data once it has been updated.

ASSET FOR COLLECTIBLES

Main characteristics

The fungibility characteristic was discussed in the last chapter, but let's take a closer look at what it means to have fungible assets.

Assets that can be traded for other units of the same asset are known as fungible assets. One Bitcoin, for example, is equivalent to any other Bitcoin in circulation, just as the Ether, Dollar and Euro are. We can also divide an asset into smaller units. These assets are virtually indistinguishable from one another.

This property is necessary for all assets to be operated using a payment mechanism. Cryptographic tokens that really are uniquely indivisible are known as non-fungible tokens. NFTs are built on contracts like ETH and DAI, but the agreement also includes important information that distinguishes each NFT from the next. Consequently, we cannot replace them with each other. It is not possible to employ a single NFT that has been broken down into smaller parts. These characteristics point to irreplaceability.

NFTs have been in the limelight for more than 8 years; however, the first ERC-721 token was not developed until 2017. Since then, a few games have grown their own NFTs as in-game objects. The most well-known example is CryptoKitties, which went viral in late

2017 because of each kitty's personality and the potential to mate and generated new versions. Despite its popularity, NFTs aren't restricted to the gaming business; other industries are beginning to see the benefits that NFTs may give.

The gaming sector is now the most popular use for NFTs. Since 2016, game developers have used open-source technologies like ERC-721 to generate NFTs on the Ethereum blockchain. However, widespread interest in these types of tokens increased in 2018.

Gaming community proved to be the pillar for building NFTs platforms. Cryptokitties has given rise to the popularity of virtual playing. But the NFTs are a new type of in-game object. NFTs have been proven to be beneficial in a variety of industries. In the case of NFTs, we can say that they are another type of in-game product. NFTs have been proven to be beneficial in a variety of industries.

Blockchain technology is used to control these digital things by registering them on the chain. Outside of the gaming industry, the primary use case for NFTs is to produce digital assets that may be utilized as a medium of exchange in other sectors.

Creating real-world assets via smart contracts is the primary application for NFTs in these businesses. Smart contracts can be used to provide digital ownership to real-world goods via NFTs. This means that instead of relying on a third party or middleman, users can swap their digital assets for tangible items outside of the virtual world.

The game sector is also interested in bringing tangible products onto the blockchain network. Because it would be a less expensive and more efficient option.

A high-quality game, for example, could feature tens of thousands of objects in its inventory. NFTs can be used to distribute these things, which can then be "leased" to users using smart contracts. Users can then link their achievements to those virtual things and buy them in the future. The most common worry about NFTs is that they will become unbalanced in the future.

This happens because they can give the same status and degree of value to any player. This means that a beginner player and a seasoned veteran may add value to the game. However, you have got options to take rid of this problem.

Complementary features

NFTs are a valuable commodity. Every token has a code that identifies it as the sole asset with a distinct digital ID. It may be used to create your digital assets and represent rare items (physical assets) with a traceable ownership tree. The opportunities to trade unique and exclusive objects, such as game components and digital art artifacts, are limitless. NFTs have a growing customer base thanks to platforms like Nifty Gateway, Open Sea and Rarible.

The following are some examples of NFT applications:

- Make Crypto or digital collectibles.

- Managing the ownership of digital things in blockchain-based games

- Allows for partial ownership of expensive goods like real estate.

- Created a digital ID system that allows users to control information from a single location.

One of the most well-known applications for NFTs to date is CryptoKitties, which is an Ethereum based game and it allows the buying, selling, and breeding the virtual cats. For the first time in two weeks, CryptoKitties, launched on November 28, 2017, saw $ 15 million in transactions with over 150,000 members. One of the CryptoKitties, which sold for $170,000, became a viral phenomenon, drawing attention to the site and Ethereum. Because of the popularity of CryptoKitties, the Ethereum network is experiencing high transaction congestion.

As a result, blockchain has gained much traction as a cutting-edge technology that provides more than simply a cryptocurrency.

Chapter 2. History of Non-fungible Tokens

Let's look at the history of non-fungible tokens, as well as their functions and applications and how they're utilized in trade. Since the inception of blockchain technology, non-fungible tokens have existed.

Bitcoin, the first cryptocurrency, produced a digital asset wholly owned by its creators. These assets were known as "bitcoins," and they provided their owners with a monetary value.

A user might hold the coins and use them to buy or sell real-world assets (mostly BTC) on the Bitcoin network. It means that these properties might be used to create fiat money on the blockchain, which had never been seen before.

This provided Bitcoin early adopters an advantage over other cryptocurrency buyers because it was evident that they could use them to buy real-world items. Bitcoin was used in the development of some of the early NFT games. For example, CryptoKitties and SOG allow their users to use their cryptocurrencies to play a game.

In 2017 and 2018, the popularity of NFTs began to skyrocket. This is just because of the use of cryptocurrency on blockchain and their growing popularity.

Until now, the main goal of the games that are based on blockchain has been to make a virtual property that can be traded for real-world properties just like fiat. However, an increasing number of players were interested in employing NFTs and other blockchain-based tools to develop enhanced gaming experiences. CryptoKitties was born as a result of this, and it was an instant hit. The investors invest on it more than $12 million by the end of 2017. At the time, this was tremendous, especially for a blockchain-based game. At the time, this was tremendous, especially for a blockchain-based game.

A CryptoKitty was said to be so expensive that a digital cat sold for $110,000. This indicates it was comparable to the cost of a work of art! This demonstrates the value of NFTs. NFTs might be used to create properties that are very useful in the existing world and also in games.

When the CryptoKitties got success, a standard was created in response to this success which is called ERC-721 standard. CryptoKitties, which introduced NFTs to a broader audience, was one of the critical reasons for the creation of this standard. This meant that individuals that had never thought of blockchain technology previously suddenly knew what it was, how it worked, and how it might be used in a game.

Non-fungible tokens can now be utilized in any game due to their ease of construction and integration. The success of NFTs has opened up a slew of new game possibilities that were previously unthinkable.

Mentioning that around these times, many games are designed to raise the value of NFTs, is also a worth statement. This is because, as already said, NFTs are much more valuable than traditional digital content and can fulfill more roles. CryptoKitties, for example, keeps track of the total number of cats made and even allows users to collect and sell them.

We will see a number more games that employ non-fungible tokens as their primary money in the near future. Players can buy things, services and other assets in the game using NFTs. These assets can include weapons and vehicles of any kind.

Myths of Non-Fungible Tokens

There are different misconceptions about non-fungible tokens. Below are some most common myths about the non-fungible tokens:

Myth #1: "There are hundreds of pending transactions on Ethereum." This is one of the most typical Ethereum misunderstandings. It demonstrates a misunderstanding of how blockchains operate and process data.

In truth, the number of pending transactions has little to do with the network's popularity or the number of people that use it. This block contains a huge number of transactions which are pending, and this is a great thing because it shows that a large number of consumers and developers are using Ethereum. As the number of people who use Ethereunm increases, Ethereum becomes more valuable.

Myth # 2: "NFTs are a rip-off" – Another prevalent misperception about NFTs is that they are a rip-off. Yet in some markets, this is true, but in the majority, it is not valid. This was true a few years ago since non-fungible tokens were foreign to most users.

However, when more people came to understand what they were, this notion faded away. For many skilled traders, NFTs and blockchain technology are now viewing as an investment instead of a fraud. In 2018 it demonstrated the fact that 9% of all NFTs were traded on the Ethereum network.

Myth # 3: "NFTs are too volatile" — Another prevalent misperception concerning non-fungible tokens is that they are excessively volatile. The price of an NFT may fluctuate just like any other token and coin. This is just because it is not stuck to a specific item, but it can be employed in various games. As a result, it can be swapped for both game things and real-world assets.

Myth # 4: "NFTs are prohibitively expensive" - This is untrue. NFTs vary in price, but on average, they are comparable to other cryptocurrencies, which are already inexpensive when compared to traditional currencies.

Myth # 5: "NFTs are too difficult to make" — Neither of these statements is correct. It's up to the game developer's choice of a blockchain platform. Developers will be able to choose from a variety of blockchain systems.

However, if they are using Ethereum, they may use NFT-Crowdfund to create their personal NFT coin. This means they won't have to learn a new programming language or design their own smart contracts to create their NFT because of a protocol. The only thing required is a basic understanding of Ethereum and how it works.

Myth # 6: "NFTs don't provide value to the gaming industry" — Another prevalent misconception about non-fungible tokens is that they don't add value to the gaming industry. If you want to gather NFTs through games, there are various games by which you can get NFTs. This indicates that these traits can boost an NFT's value. NFTs, after all, can be used in a variety of ways, including as virtual objects in games like CryptoKitties and Spells of Genesis.

Problems or Controversies

You'll find some overlapping difficulties, such as ecological, logistical, and ethical ones, as you peel back the first layer of NFTs. Many have pointed out the consequences of NFT development and trade explosions on worlds that have already been wrecked by climate change (severe ecological impact) (climate change-related disasters, environment, racism, inequality).

Is there any connection present between NFTs and global warming? Simply put, the process of producing NFTs, adding tokens to the blockchain, and the wave of transactions consume a lot of energy (bidding, resale, etc.). When you multiply it by a massive market driven by greed, you get new kinds of environmental damage.

Ether is a platform that has a stable blockchain with a high number of these NFTs. This was supposed to turn the device into a dioxide one while protecting it to use, but that hasn't happened yet. This switch's time is still uncertain.

From a justice and ethical sense, selling a particular piece of art as an NFT may not be the best option. If the work of a developing artist is not adequately enforced or scrutinized to see if it is authentic, it can be horribly exploited. It all relies on the game creator and the blockchain platform they employ.

Developers have the ability to use any blockchain platform of their choice because there are various varieties available. The person who writes the NFT is the authentic artist, the actual creator or the owner of the copyright. It has created an atmosphere in which cryptocurrency transactions' relative anonymity can be exploited, stolen, and hurt.

Make enlightened business decisions

It is necessary to have careful business planning and also a selection of art galleries and dealers for transitioning from traditional art to cryptographic art. In terms of sales volume with Nifty Gateway dominating, the crypto art market is now worth $445 million.

Because the competition is fierce, it's vital to learn the jargon, select the right platform, and get advice from knowledgeable people. Do not try to put too much emphasis in order to making a wise or rapid profit just yet. It is not recommended that proceeds from the sale of cryptographic arts be used to pay rent. As a result, it will be similar to the "old" art market.According to studies, the footprint a computer requires to construct a single board NFT is the same as the whole electricity usage of EU citizens in a month, given the environmental impact of Ether mining.

For the year 2020, the Louvre Museum used the same amount of electricity as 677,224 Paris households. It may be good for to put set of the money got from cryptography into NFT grants of Jason Bailey's and other efforts to decrease NFT power use.

Try with one piece at a time, just when you're with a new medium. Activated encrypted art can be finished, embedded, or produced by playing it back in media, such as a motion in.mp4 or.gif format, adding music, or converting a photo into interactive digital art.

You can also make an NFTonly series to determine which of your works is the most popular. While staying true to your beliefs and the brand community, we explore and research what's ideal for your target collector and you.

As a result, as long as the legal implications are understood, NFT can be a compelling alternative to the traditional art market. The market and the specific artwork to be sold are chosen after careful analysis of commercial, practical and legal factors.

Chapter 3. Cases of use of Non-fungible Token

Gaming

NFT is well-known in the gaming community since it overcomes one of the game's intrinsic issues. Rare skins, weaponry, equipment and functions are restricted in popular games like Fortnite, pubg, COD etc. These capabilities can be readily transferred and used in several games with NFT. As a result, non-fungible tokens contribute to the game's economy.

Digital Assets

Decentraland participants can acquire virtual land. Another local example is ENS, which employs NFTs in the ETH area to make selling and purchasing easier.

Identity

NFTs are ideal for preventing identity theft since they can digitize personal information such as appearance, medical records and educational background. Digital artists can also transform their creations to NFT for copyright reasons.

NFTs can be used to turn actual game tickets into non-fungible tokens, allowing for the detection of fakes.

Collectibles

NFT is ushering in a new era in the realm of collectibles. Traditional collectors have been changed into digital products as a response.

It's worth looking at the standards and origins of non-fungible tokens to get a better understanding of how they're used, which brings us back to ERC721. You may find a list of applications of the most common NFT.

The best question is, why hasn't the NFT between finance, technology, sports, the arts and music been sold? Soon, all of the well-known names will join the game. For example, Twitter creator Jack Dorsey sold his first post for $ 2.9 million on March 22. "I was just setting up my Twitter," the tweet read. The funds were donated to a worthy cause.

A team of NFTs and art lovers got a piece of Bansky's art, burnt it down, and resold it as an NFT artwork for around US$380,000. Lindsay Lohan's first NFT, "Lindsay 'Lightning' Lohan," was sold on rarible.com for around $50,000 (she also promised to contribute the earnings to a charity that accepts Bitcoin to empower young people).

A limited-edition NFC tournament trading card of Rob Gronkowski was sold for more than a million dollars. Elon Musk has changed his choice to selling an NFT based on a techno song about NFTs. The limited art collection of Steve Aoki (Dream Catcher) sold for $4.25 million, and there are still many works available for purchase.

Let's not forget that adding/listing "each" of your NFT works to the Ethereum network would set you back $100. Unless you are already well-known, you may only receive one or two bucks in exchange for a $100 listing.

What are ERC-721 tokens?

The ERC-721 coin is designed to meet the needs of the Ethereum platform's intelligent contracts. Dieter Shirley, a developer, proposed the formation of this new standard at the end of 2017, and it has attracted a lot of attention in the crypto community since then.

As previously stated, this standard was created to generate interchangeable tokens with unique and non-expendable properties, ensuring that each token is unique throughout its lifetime and cannot be deteriorated or destroyed.

The phrase ERC-721 relates to the creation of non-fungible tokens (NFTs) on the Ethereum Blockchain as a way of establishing guiding principles. As a result, NTF is a type of token made in compliance with the Ethereum ERC-721 definition.

NFTs may be found in a wide variety of distributed networks, such Neo and EOS, in addition to the Ethereum blockchain. But on the other hand, such systems need intelligent contractability and a full set of NFT techniques. Smart contracts, for example, allow for the inclusion of specific descriptions, such as metadata, in the agreement.

Important Information

NFT Art

Non-fungible tokens (NFTs) have been used by visual artists to generate NFT art. One reason for the growing demand of this particular NFT market is the amount of money that artists may recoup in NFT markets.

Crypto Art Data

The entire amount of NFT-based artwork will exceed $ 8.2 million by the end of 2020, according to a crypto art data and analysis platform that focuses on Cryptocurrency's art. When compared to the prior monthly volume of $ 2.6 million dollars, this was a significant increase.

The market is actually worth more than $ 130 billion. Collectors' concept of collecting has shifted from a simple recreational activity to a severe financial movement, as seen by the increase in market value.

According to Richard Chen, the inventor of Crypto art, a rise in understanding of what non-fungible tokens can accomplish to ensure authenticity has contributed to an increase in the volume of negotiations.

Artists working with digital media, principally, will be able to sell their work for some of their greatest rates in the last months of 2020. If the value of Bitcoin fluctuates, a digital artwork created with NFT advanced technologies will be valued 262 ETHEREUM.

An NFT developer arranged the purchase of the product, which was NFT's highest object at the period but hasn't been sold until several months later, for $131.250 earlier this year.

Surprisingly, the most OK days for NFT artists were still ahead of them, as a collection of NFT artworks sold for $ 777,777.78 just two months following the auction.

The value of each token is determined by its rarity and distinctiveness, as evidenced by this significant fluctuation in value. Non-fungible token apps like Decentraland, CryptoKitties, CryptoPunks and others are in high demand as a result.

What are the Cryptokitties?

Cryptokitties, a popular game based on the ETH-Powered decentralized network, allows users to collect virtual cats, sell them to other players, and reproduce them.

Since its update at the height of that year's bull race, the blockchain of the 1990s Cult Classic Tamagotchi (in the very same spirit, check out Defi's Aavegotchi!), which has provided as a starting point for newbies since its release at the peak of that year's bull race, has gone on to serve as a bastion of NFT.

The first general use case in the biggest blockchain blocks devoted to leisure activities was this game. Furthermore, the event opened the prospect of DAPPs used for aesthetic reasons.

Cryptokitties sparked a lot of enthusiasm on the Ethereum platform when it first launched, but its popularity rapidly turned into a negative when it slowed down the network, causing prices to rise and transaction confirmations to take longer than intended.

Smart contracts may be used by Kitties and virtual cat breeders to market their virtual pets. Non-fungible token (NFT) exchanges like OpenSea attract real money and investors.

If you adore cats and want to learn how to buy Cryptokitties, the process is straightforward. You'll need to have a Chrome or Mozilla internet browser, a MetaMask account, as well as some Ether (ETH) tokens to get started. Then head to the Kittie's Market to select your kitty. After that, simply pay for it, and you're done.

Dapper Technologies, the company founded Cryptokitties, has recently introduced NBA Topshot, a digital memorabilia market intended particularly towards NBA fans.

What Are CryptoPunks?

A terrifying Cryptopunks "Alien" NFT Got Renowned IN JAN 2021 Since It Was Managed to sell FOR AN AWESOME $ 760,000, which was at the time was the equal of 605 Ethereum.

Cryptopunks is known for being the first NFT series, and its groundbreaking concept predates both the Cryptokitties and ERC-721 blockchains, which were both launched in the same year. Consequently, shortage has grown, including an average sale price of $6,000 in 2020.

Digital art, according to a spokesman for the investment group, which includes several notable members of the DEFI industry, would attract a new generation of collectors who will appreciate it over time and turn it into "iconic" digital works The question "punk," number 2890, is one of Larva Labs' nine existing "alien" collections, and it was last issued in July 2017 for only 8 ETHE (about $1,500 at the time).

What we can convert to NFT

Yield Farming in Defi

NFTs are starting to collide with decentralized finance (DEFI), particularly agricultural practices that produce products and services.

The fruits of this new alliance did not appear in the marketplace until 2020. For example, the Yearn Finance protocol, which is a DEFI protocol, has created an insurance product named Y. Y.

Insure displays the unique aspects of insurance contracts using NFT methods (ERC-721). When used to communicate the exact characteristics of an insurance policy, most ERC-20 Tokens "didn't make sense." Defi's other companies include Enjin, Bancor and Meme. They have an NFT aspect to them.

Individual skills

Non-fungible tokens can be used to show a person's ability to monetize them in the future. An NFT can be used to play movies, podcasts and bulletins, among other things.

Some Famous NFT Projects

As collected and marketable components, NFTs are useful in a variety of applications. A selection of the most well-known will be provided below.

DecentraLand.

Decentraland is a randomized vr ecosystem in which individuals, among other things, may trade and own digital land. Cryptovoxels is a game in which participants exchange, produce, and create virtual assets.

Gods Unchained

This is a poker game where the cards are recorded on the blockchain as NFT. Because each digital card is unique, players can possess and trade them on the same level as physical cards.

My Crypto Heroes

It's an online character game where players may elevate historical figures by completing tasks and eliminating other gamers. Tokens stored on the Ethereum Blockchain reflect the game's goods and heroes.

Binance Collectibles

They're non-fungible tokens (NFTs) developed in partnership with ENJIN and BINANCE for a specific use case. Keep an eye out for our forthcoming raffles and follow Binance on Twitter if you want to get your hands on one.

Crypto stamps

These were provided by the Austrian Post Office to help bridge the gap between the physical and digital worlds. These stamps, like any other, are used to transport mail and goods. Their automated images, on the other hand, are stored on the Ethereum Network, giving them a valuable digitized collection.

Top NFT Projects

The number of NFT-related activities and items has expanded in lockstep with the exponential growth of the NFT subspace. They include everything from casino companies to NTF-affiliated commercial facilities. These are the top five NFT efforts in the works right now.

OpenSea:

The majority of NFT items and art are sold on a commercial basis here. ENS, virtual pets and property plots are among the objects that have been reported. Surprisingly, purchases can be made using a few virtual currencies such as DAI and ETH in the commercial section.

Async.Art

It's a programmable art marketplace run by NFT.

Its unique feature is that the artist can produce dynamic art in which the master art is built of multiple layers, each of which can be altered.

The master refers to the entire piece, while the layers refer to the individual layers or elements that make it up. Customers can buy the master or individual "layers."

By modifying different layers, the artist can allow specific parameters of the work to be modified. The various variations of the layers are referred to as states.

Color, scale, rotation, transparency and other factors can be changed in each state within the artist's limitations. Only the owner of a state has the ability to change it, and his changes are immediately reflected in the master.

It's also feasible to make adjustments based on variables like time, stock market trends and weather. As a result, the art will be "alive" and alter over time.

CryptoKitties:

Despite the fact that we have already covered this assignment, it deserves to be included on the list of the best NFT projects because it has elevated the entire NFT game.

Ethereum Name Service (ENS):

This is a project that started in the middle of 2017 to manage area names. The ETH domain names are non-fungible tokens (NFTs) that adhere to the Ethereum ERC-721 specifications and may be purchased on commercial NFT exchanges.

Latest Sells of NFTs

NFT sold a column from 'The New York Times' for 475,000 euros.

Kevin Roose, a New York Times journalist, has sold a New York Times column at auction for $ 560,000 (approximately 475,000 euros) after converting it into an NFT (non-fungible token), a blockchain-based certification system for digital authenticity that has recently starred in some spectacular auctions, including the sale of the first tweet for nearly 2.5 million euros and digital artistic composition for approximately 58 million euros.

The sale of Roose's column is entirely non-profit. It is indicated in the same column that has been auctioned, which consists of describing the column's online auction endeavor itself, that the proceeds of the sale will be donated to The New York Times' Neediest Cases Fund.

Roose wondered if the phenomenon of the NFTs brought to art or the sale of NBA plays on film could be used to journalism, so he consulted the newspaper and started it as an experiment.

According to the author, he chose to take the test after witnessing how digital certificates were being used in numerous industries, particularly in the art world:

The column details the steps involved in creating the sale, which lasted 24 hours and had a minimum price of 0.5 Ether (a cryptocurrency similar to bitcoin), which is around $ 850. The ultimate figure was 350 Ether.

Even if they spent nearly half a million euros, the buyer of the first column would not have the copyright to the piece or any rights to reproduce or retransmit it. It will simply be a PNG picture with the column's property title. As a bonus, Roose offered to publish the buyer's name and send him a personalized voice note from The Daily presenter Michael Barbaro congratulating him on his purchase.

In his piece, Roose adds, "The world of cryptocurrency is replete with crooks whose schemes frequently fail." Furthermore, opponents believe that crypto-related initiatives and NFTs consume a lot of power and computer processing power, posing a risk to the planet as they grow rapidly. "What exactly NFT clients get for their payment," adds the author, "and if those tokens would become error messages if the marketplaces and hosting companies that contain the underlying data vanish."

"It's easy to be dubious of NFTs," Rose writes in her piece. "However, I'm cautiously positive about them," he says, "since they provide a new method for creative people to make a career online."

Expensive NFTs

NFT supporters believe the NFT Ethereum (ETH) space has a lot of potential. Criticism, on the other side, argues that the NFT market is overvalued and that the hoopla surrounding non-fungible tokens is merely hype. NFTs, on the other hand, are already being sold for huge sums. Let's take a look at some of the most expensive non-fungible tokens currently available.

Beeple's Digital Art Collection - $ 3.5 million

Mike Winkelmann, a CGI artist in the group known as Beeple, achieved the most significant sales in NFT's history. People started it all with a tweet announcing the sale of 21 of his paintings. Things went rapidly because his work was concentrated on NFTs. All of this was supported by records and a precise sample of Beeple hair.

The 'Winklevoss Brothers Gemini Exchange' received a portion of the sales proceeds from the NFT Nifty Gateway Marketplace. The first ten auctions brought in about $900,000. Bidders paid a total of $1.2 million for ten additional works of art.

The last painting's auction was announced just as it was about to begin. Tim Kang sold it at auction for $ 777,777. 21 works of art were sold for a total of $3.5 million. Following the deal, the artist posted a video on Twitter in which his friends welcomed Beeple's performance with a shower of Champagne in celebration of their victory.

Rick and Morty ($ 2.3 million)

Justin Roiland, who created the famous animated comedy "Rick and Morty," was one of the artists who overcharged for NFT artwork. His 16-piece collection was auctioned for ETH 1,300 (about $2.3 million). Roiland noted in a statement that the auction was a way for him to push the boundaries of cryptographic art while simultaneously donating a percentage of the proceeds to help destitute individuals living on the streets of Los Angeles.

It's also worth mentioning that some of Roiland's artwork has been replicated. The works "It's Tree Guy Basically" and "Eligible Bachelors" are $10 and $100, respectively. Works of art made in a single copy sold for a higher price due to their rarity and originality—the play "The Simpsons" sold for $ 290,100. The opening offer for the auction was $ 14,999, and its counterpart was sold for the same amount.

Axie Infinity Lands- $ 1.5 million

Users can establish their own kingdom in Axie Infinity, complete with fascinating characters. Lucia is the name of the world's virtual property marketplace, and there are just a few slots left. The land is divided into 90,601 smaller portions, with players controlling 19% of them.

Falcon claims that the land he bought is in a great location. Furthermore, the trend is gradually developing, as seen by the expanding number of active users on Axie Infinity. It would also be feasible to arrange future activities in "your area," such as concerts or festivals, and benefit from them.

One F1 Delta Time track

F1 Delta Time's region was sold for nearly nine million REVV tokens. At the time of writing, the REVV had risen by 500 percent, and producing the same quantity of REVV would cost $ 1.2 million at the current exchange rate.

There are 330 of these tokens in all, separated into four grades ranging from "Rare" to "Apex." These tokens are used to create the virtual circuit for the Circuit de Monaco. Each token includes a virtual track share as well as other perks. This particular NFT had reached the pinnacle of its evolution. Its buyer will receive 5% of all in-game sales and 4.2 percent of elite staking revenue generated by player deposits. Both can be paid for with REVV utility tokens.

Finance Insurance for NFT

A separate digital policy will protect you up to 5,000 ETHagainst Curve's smart contract mistakes. NFT costs 350 ETH, which is worth about $ 560,000 right now. Yinsure is also known as the cover. In a nutshell, it's a hybrid between Nexus Mutual-backed insurance and another type of tokenized insurance. The letter NFT is used to identify insurance plans. Each is a one-of-a-kind NFT, that may be sold, traded, or bought.

Virtual lands in Decentraland

Someone paid 514 ETH for 12,600 m2 on the Decentraland blockchain game. The game is based on Ethereum and is a decentralized virtual reality platform. On the platform, users may create, play with, and monetize their content and applications. In Decentraland, LAND is a simple 3D virtual space. This non-fungible digital asset is managed by Ethereum smart contracts, and the virtual landowner has complete control over it.

Land at 22.2 in Decentraland is available for purchase for 345 ETH.

In the area of technology, Decentraland has made a comeback. Another 22.2-acre parcel in an "excellent location" is available for grabs. In Decentraland, the size of the land is fixed. The majority of Decentraland's space is sold or leased, with roughly 80% of it being private. The remaining land, such as roads and squares, is owned by no one.

Players can only stroll their avatars on their own property or on public ground, so picking the correct spot is crucial. Lots in more popular neighborhoods are likely to be more expensive than those in less popular areas.

Based on the rise in non-fungible tokens and sales, this could be another major trend soon following DeFi. Another amazing feature of NFTs is that they each have their own unique characteristics. While NFTs are still small businesses, they have a wide range of applications.

Crypto Space Commanders Battle cruiser - 250 ETH

It's a space MMORPG created by Lucid Sight. The company collected a total of $ 11 million to support the creation of its "scarcity engine," a technology that would allow it to quickly launch its Cryptocurrency games to smartphones, PCs and consoles.

Cryptocurrency acceptance will be aided by video games. Ethereum is used to protect the game's assets, execute all in-game contracts, and power the game's free-market economy, which runs without the need for a developer.

In order to find materials, users can either explore the world or participate in combat with other players. Players can benefit from their resources by trading, keeping, or selling them at any point along their voyage.

Each ship in the game is distinct and has its own set of characteristics, which you may discover through playing the game. The more valuable a ship is in terms of earning wealth in the game, the more expensive it is to buy it. When the Battlecruiser initially arrived on the market in September of 2020, it cost 250 ETH.

The Battlecruiser was the first combat ship of its kind ever built in the world. It can be moved quickly anywhere on the CSC globe within 20 light-years, making it excellent for sneaking up on enemy ships and launching a deadly ambush.

Gods Unchained (Atlas) -210 ETH

It's a competitive card game based on the Ethereum Blockchain that's comparable in gameplay and principles to the enormously successful game Hearthstone.

The most major distinction between the two is Gods Unchained's exclusive mechanics, which are enabled by the game's Blockchain-based structure. If players so desire, they can resell their cards on the secondary market. Gods Unchained is the world's first Blockchain-based e-sport, and it is now in beta testing. There will be an annual Gods Unchained World Championship, with a prize fund of $100,000 and 10% of all card pack sales going to the winner. The prize pool for the first Gods Unchained event is currently anticipated to be around USD$540,865.

Because the game contains an e-sport component, players want to be as competitive as possible when playing in tournaments. Thus, they build strong decks that increase the value of the cards.

The Gods Unchained team will issue a maximum of four "Mythic" cards per year, each with powerful abilities in the game. Atlas represents the god of the sky and is one of the Mythic cards. It was found in a deck of cards by chance by a lucky player who had no idea how precious it was.

However, it wasn't until the Gods Unchained team assured the card's owner of the digital treasure's worth that the item piqued their interest.

The auction took five days to complete, with the winning bidder getting 210 ETH. Only time will tell whether this is a successful investment, but the early signs are encouraging.

Gods Unchained (Prometheus) -235 ETH

The marketplace in Gods Unchained was presented after much anticipation, resulting in a frenzy of activity as players began exchanging cards.

An additional mythical card, known as the Prometheus, was hidden in a random package with a one in a million chance of being discovered. Given the card's one-of-a-kind qualities as well as its overall game strength, it was the ideal card for those serious about battling for a piece of the $ 500,000 prize pool.

As a result, when the player who discovered Prometheus put the card up for sale, it was in high demand, fetching a peak offer of 235 Ethereum at an auction.

Chapter 4. Security and Non-fungible Token

Standards for Non-Fungible Token

Non-fungible tokens are incredibly powerful due to their requirements. They not only provide developers confidence that assets will behave in a certain way, but they also explain how to interact with the assets' core functionality.

This means that programmers can construct complex logic that can be applied to assets and made available to people who may not know how to interact with them. Interoperability across several NFT games is also possible thanks to standards, which opens up the prospect of asset trade (cross-game).

There are four key standards that enable NFTs to function, and only one group is currently interested in developing NFT standards: the ERC-721 (Non-Fungible Token Standard).

This standard was designed in 2018 by AGAME, a blockchain-based game platform. The purpose of this standard is to establish a set of universal rules and functionality that can be used in any game that uses NFTs.

This enables cross-game compatibility and encourages developers to utilize this as the primary NFT standard. Although some other groups have begun to develop standards, none have yet been formally released. As a result, ERC-721 is one of the few standards that supports NFTs and allows them to work together seamlessly.

Some designers base their design decisions on cultural conventions and beliefs. If NFTs are allowed to resemble real-world assets, they can become part of these norms and values.

For example, certain Japanese communities have a particular perspective on non-fungible things (the same is true for many others around the world).

Chopsticks and paper, for example, are considered unique and valued in Japan because of the labor that went into making them.

If game designers use NFTs to include this cultural element into their games, they will be able to build game assets that are more valuable than what players can create on their own.

One way that NFTs may outperform traditional digital products is in this area. Blockchain technology is where NFTs' true promise resides. They can either operate together or be utterly incompatible, depending on the blockchains they run on and the tools given by developers.

In the last year, a lot of effort has gone into making NFTs and other blockchain technologies work together so that game developers can gain more benefits and gamers can earn more money. This includes the requirement for a large number of characters to do specific tasks, such as avatars, that may be transferred to other game players.

NFTs are really simple to make. The only need is that you give it a set of characteristics, such as a name and an image.

These features can then be used in the NFT's smart contract, which will take care of the rest and ensure that it works with other NFTs. NFTs are created using ERC-721-compliant smart contracts.

NFTs have been formally recognized by the Ethereum network and are thus classified as blockchain assets. This means they have their own address and identification number, allowing them to be managed just like any other asset.

The only distinction is that the NFT will always be a one-of-a-kind piece. This, like fiat money, gives them a certain measure of value and significance. For example, if someone makes an NFT for their game character, the player can utilize it as a type of game cash.

This incentivizes them to treat the NFT like cash, exchanging it for real-world goods and services within the game (fiat).

The Ethereum blockchain is the most common means to get non-fungible tokens. Even though NFTs are supported by a number of different projects, the ERC-721 standard ensures that they work seamlessly on Ethereum.

The key advantage is that the blockchain contains all of the necessary tools and requirements for establishing an NFT. This means that developers are greatly driven to design their own ERC-721 smart contracts so that gamers can easily use them.

The fundamental functionality, specifying its attributes, and the token interface are the three essential aspects of an NFT contract's smart contract.

The primary function of an NFT is covered in the first section. When a token is generated and exists within a game, this refers to what it can do. This could, for example, detail how a specific item can be used to advance in the game or what special skills it possesses.

Non-Fungible Tokens Metadata

The smart contract has three basic sections, as previously mentioned, and stating its attributes is the second key part of the smart contract.

There is a list of attributes in the non-fungible token smart contract that specify the NFT qualities. Its name and ID are among them. The following attribute is "metadata." This is information about the NFT that isn't included in its properties. "Owner," "location," and "avatar" are some of the attributes that can be used with this type of metadata.

The owner field specifies who is responsible for storing and tracking the NFT in question. This could be a user or a game creator. This is beneficial since it holds the owner of an NFT accountable for any acts made with respect to it, such as transferring it to another player or destroying it.

The next field is the location, which could have a variety of meanings and interpretations depending on the type of game being produced, as some game mechanics may be dependent on having this information available.

"Location," for example, could simply refer to the position of an object in a scene. It could also relate to a game's item's position in relation to other game items. It's possible that an item has a unique "location" that governs whether it's okay to interact with it. It may be used to explain an item's current state.

The metadata field is used to specify any additional information about an NFT that isn't included in the properties or determined by other attributes like name and picture. Factors like creation time, creator and image ID can be included in this information.

The token interface is the last section of the NFT smart contract. This refers to the various ways in which smart contracts can interact with an NFT.

It is beneficial to game creators since it allows them to construct new NFTs without having to form any variations to their existing code. They can use the token interface to construct a new "monster" (for example) and assign it a battle power. They can then add these details to the metadata of the NFT.

This means that new objects can be made without the need for certain points or levels to be established. This offers more possibilities in terms of game mechanics and design, enhancing the power and utility of smart contracts.

Be smart about copyright.

Copyright is a core of intellectual property, especially when it comes to NFTs, and any artist should understand how and when to use it.

In the United States, it is not essential to register with the copyright office in order to exist; nonetheless, it is necessary to apply against others.

The Copyright Act of 1976 allows writers of photographs, sculptures or graphics to reproduce, distribute, and produce their works exclusively. Platforms must develop techniques for dealing with threatening items. However, recording a visual arts work in a few minutes, ideally before it is published, is simple.

While it may be tempting to convert old photos into NFTs without significant changes and a clear supplementary message, doing so without doing so is like walking on a tightrope. Converting a digital artwork without the author's consent may lead to legal action, with the offender claiming that the use is "fair" under copyright law.

Courts will evaluate the similarity between the source and defendant's work, the marketplace in which the companies operate, and the defendant's work's purpose and transformational character when making fair-use rulings.

A licensing agreement can help you avoid problems and give you a great way to communicate with other creators.

Furthermore, artists should be told that the NFT purchaser does not have the right to copy the underlying work purchased from them until a written agreement between the client and the artist is signed.

Any NFT platform can grant itself a non-exclusive, worldwide, and royal family license to disseminate and reproduce copies of the work for sale by implementing the platform's Terms and Conditions. Unfortunately, these parameters are almost never, if ever, negotiated.

Keeping your information safe

Linking an NFT to an Ether-accepting platform is critical for artists. Software wallets (such as Meta-Mask or Coinbase) and hardware wallets can both digital store currencies (like a hard drive).

Hardware wallets are a better long-term investment that has been proven to be more trustworthy due to greater protection against hacking (internet fraud).

Look for two-factor authentication, a safe place to store your seed phrase (which is the same as your password), and the ability to send and receive payments when choosing a bitcoin wallet (same as a debit card number).

When trading cryptocurrencies, it's also a good idea to get into the habit of using a virtual private network (VPN). Before developing their own wallet, artists should check whether wallets are accepted by the NFT platform (for example, Foundation uses MetaMask).

NFT Risks and Scams & How to Avoid them

The NFT craze is real, with several popular models fetching hundreds of dollars. While the NFT area is fascinating, we must also take a step back and consider the hazards. As Garyvee pointed out on Twitter, 97-99 percent of NFT projects will fail; therefore, learning and patience are essential. We must also analyze and discuss the drawbacks.

NFT Major Trading Risks

Buying A ReplicaFake Banksy is said to have made over $1 million in ETH from the NFT sales in February 2020. The branding and non-fungible tokens for the "Pest Supply" account were done in Banksy's distinctive graffiti-stencil style.

Some people believed they had gotten a good deal, with one saying, "I either just blew $750 or got the deal of a lifetime on Banksy." However, because there is no authentic Banksy NFT on Rarible, this person purchased a phony Banksy.

We must pause and consider whether we are getting the actual bargain. This is comparable to how traditional artworks are created. For instance, if you had a Picasso that you believe is genuine and that everyone believes genuine, it will be worth millions of dollars.

What happens, however, if you have a professional come in to test it and they discover it isn't true?

That painting now has a value of five dollars. The same thing is happening in the realm of NFT; individuals are falling for this scam, and it is likely to continue.

For an article headed "NFT morons," this account's records revealed hundreds of sales to purchasers ranging from 0.116 Ethereum to over 60 Ethereum. If you don't want to be the morons, research the NFT you're planning to buy, especially the valuable ones.

It's not that difficult. You just need to go to this piece's page and look at its history, including when it was sold and who bid on it across all platforms.

You may notice that a false account only has roughly 300 followers; however, this is in no way representative of the real Banksy account.

If you're a fan of King, you can also look for this account in the platform's search bar. You can also double-check or cross-check on social media if any other profiles appear.

Almost all of these folks have a reputation, and it's for a good reason. They'll most likely be on Instagram, Twitter, Facebook and other social media platforms. You can probably find the link to those people's NFTs on their social media pages, which will redirect you to the previous pages of the market. You may now check to see if these are genuine NFT accounts.

If you find something that seems too inexpensive and from a well-known artist, it's a red sign. If you come across a person of influence selling an NFT for 15 ETH, take a moment to verify their profile, history and cross-reference with other social media.

Liquid Market

The NFT market is often illiquid, which is one of its main drawbacks. While having a look at the crypto market, we see that they are a lot more liquid, which implies that if you buy Crypto and things go bad, you can sell a quarter of all of it.

Right now, you will not be able to do that in the NFT universe. It's a one-size-fits-all proposition. When we look at cryptocurrency, we can see that it gradually builds up support levels.

The bitcoin charts, for example, feature moving averages, and we have a lot of historical data to show us where this cryptocurrency might be valued in the future. So, even if it begins to decline, we will be able to withdraw gradually, so, even if it starts to fall, we may gradually work our way out of our predicament.

However, pricing for these NFTs has no support level in the realm of NFT art or gaming. They can go from having no money to having $100,000 in a matter of hours. One crypto punk sold for almost $700,000, but when we look at its history, we can notice that it was only sold twice: for around $2,000 and again for around $700,000. There were offers in between these transactions, which is how it ended up at such a high price.

Checking the NFTs' value history is crucial. Is the NFT a one-day wonder, or has it grown in value over time?

It's hazardous because if you invest $1,000 or $5,000 in an NFT and the market tanks, you won't be able to simply exit your position. Under the illiquid market, it's practically all or nothing. When things go bad, just a few people will be interested in buying your NFT, which you paid thousands of dollars for.

You might not get anything in return for that NFT. So, if you're ready to buy the NFT, go back and review the history to see what the previous sale prices, bids and transfers were like.

Wash Trades

This occurs when someone creates an NFT, advertises it for sale, and then buys it back for a high price, giving the impression that it is a popular NFT. For example, if you notice an NFT was sold for 500 ETH, but you check the history and discover it was only formed five days ago and is now being sold for 500 ETH, you should be suspicious.

If you look at the trading history of the genuine ones, you'll notice that they didn't magically move from zero to one thousand dollars overnight. There are numerous offers along the route, and we'll watch how the price rises.

Also, if you find an account with a lot of offers and sales coming from odd addresses that no one can verify, it's probably a wash sale.

To summarize, when you're out in the NFT realm, exercise extreme caution. When purchasing an NFT, make careful to look into the NFT's history and verify the originator.

NFT Scams You Must Avoid

Common Crypto Scams

If you fall for these NFTs frauds, all your wealth will be gone. Imagine visiting a MetaMask site that you googled, and it turns out to be a phishing link; you'll lose everything you put into that false wallet right away.

For NFT artists, the situation is significantly worse. You must establish a reputation in the NFT art world, and your reputation is inextricably related to your address. For example, on Rarible's first page, you'll find a list of the top sellers from the last 30 days, along with their addresses.

Let's imagine you've created a reputation, put in a lot of effort, and over the last 30 years; you've made it to the top seller's list but, all of a sudden, your wallet has been hacked, and you can no longer use it. Unless you have a million followers, this is a really difficult thing to re-establish.

If you're Mark Cuban and your wallet was hacked, you're in trouble. You may just go to Twitter and inform your followers that your wallet has been hijacked, along with a link to your new wallet's new address. If you're a rising artist or a newcomer to the NFT scene, you may have been working and struggling for over a year to establish a reputation.

Suddenly, the address you constructed, as well as the reputation associated with it, is in jeopardy. You can't use that wallet anymore, and things are only getting worse. You can establish royalties on NFT, for example, if you make art and set a 10% or

20% royalty for every time NFT is resold. The revenues will be returned to the wallet that founded the NFT. So, if you formed a wallet, established a reputation, sold NFTs, and are receiving royalties on those royalties, those royalties will be returned to the original wallet.

If your wallet has been hacked or you have fallen victim to this phishing scam, someone now has access to your wallet, and you cannot use it. It's time for you to move on.

This is just a piece of cake of what happens in the crypto realm. Scams abound in the crypto industry. Scammers will seek out money wherever it is available. The crypto space's ecology is brimming with cash. Phishing links might also be sent to your email address.

You may receive a hoax from "Ledger" claiming that you've been locked out of your wallet and requesting your 12 or 24-word seed phrase.

Never, ever, ever, EVER, EVER, EVER, EVER, NEVER! The only time your seed phrases will be used in Crypto is when you begin it. You should always remember yourself as the one who creates or restores a ledger wallet or any other wallet. So, if you receive an email, it's most likely a fraud.

It's also visible on exchanges like Coinbase. Fake Coinbase emails claim that you have been locked out of your account and that you must update your password by clicking this link. It's a phishing attempt. So, if you receive an email and you are not the one who sent it, proceed with caution.

If you ever receive something from a site like Coinbase, it may or may not be genuine; however, the way to check this is not by opening the link you were sent but rather by entering the app the conventional way.

Do not reply to emails or click on links that you did not send.

Crypto Giveaway Scams

At least $587,000 has been stolen from victims as a result of 'The Elon Musk cryptocurrency giveaway scams. This is one of the most popular sorts of cryptocurrency scams, and it's particularly common on social media sites like Twitter and YouTube.

How do they work?

The hacker will pose as a well-known company or public figure and claim to be giving away cryptocurrency. If you wish to participate in these giveaways, you must first pay a certain quantity of cryptocurrency to the address provided. They frequently offer to return double, triple, or even more of what you sent.

They want you to believe that if you don't do this, you will be missing out on a huge opportunity. They usually state the precise amount of cryptocurrency to be given away, such as "100,000 BTC giveaway." Then they'll post false comments to make it appear as if other individuals are receiving the coins.

Their goal is to make you fear missing out and donate bitcoin to the scammers before you have a chance to think about whether or not this offer is genuine.

YouTube and Twitter Giveaways

You can watch live stream videos of a firm or a celebrity talking about something completely unrelated to NFT and Crypto on YouTube. However, the comment section is filled with bots claiming to have won a prize. Some bogus giveaway accounts may even have blue verified check marks on Twitter to make them appear more authentic. Some bots will respond to tweets by saying that the freebies are genuine and that they have just received them. They're attempting to establish "social proof" that the gifts are genuine.

Protecting Yourself

Almost all crypto or NFT giveaways have so far proven to be scams.

These phoney giveaways all follow a similar pattern: they pretend to be someone else and then ask you to transfer bitcoin before giving you more. The best approach to protect yourself is to educate yourself and learn how to spot a scam like this.

You can't get your money back because crypto transactions are irrevocable. As a result, once your cryptocurrency is transmitted to those phoney giveaway addresses, it is lost forever. This is also why this type of con is so successful and keeps repeating itself.

The bottom takeaway is that anything that sounds too wonderful to be true is almost certainly a ruse. Before you send your Crypto to others, think twice.

What's Next for NFTs?

NFT's potential and possibilities are limitless, and recent record-breaking sales are helping to propel the technology forward. At the same time, there's a roadblock in the way of wider adoption: less knowledge of blockchain and crypto technologies. "If you can educate people and allow them to get a taste of it, they may not be afraid by it," said John G. Fields, the developer of Grow Your Base.

This education includes security. Newcomers to the blockchain realm must learn how to keep their wallets and private keys secure so that their precious digital assets are not compromised by hackers.

Many NFTs and digital assets might be extremely valuable due to their scarcity and rarity. Without a doubt, losing them will cause some headaches. To safeguard their assets, authors and developers of digital assets must include solid licensing and copyrighting provisions in smart contracts. So far, the bulk of existing crypto wallets has proven to be extremely tough and complex to use for mainstream novices and new users.

Enjin Wallet, Pillar Wallet and Wax Cloud Wallet are just a few examples of wallets that are always being developed and launched with the goal of improving this.

NGRAVE ZERO is another wallet worth noticing. It's built to be the most secure and "coldest" crypto wallet that's also smooth and user-friendly, so you can interact with your NFTs with confidence. In a safe and secure environment, users can exchange and keep their digital assets.

NGRAVE also has a high-resolution touch screen, which has the potential to allow owners to show off their digital assets to others from a mobile device.

Another component of public education is to make people aware of how nerdy, technical, and even geeky blockchain and NFTs are.

It is required to reduce this even further in order to make it accessible and usable for people with less technical know-how. Dr.Jesse Reich, the CEO of the Netherlands, claimed that the problem "lies in making blockchain invisible to novice users while remaining accessible to advanced users."

Although some NFT projects, such as CryptoKitties, have effectively introduced new people to the blockchain, and the current rise and development of NFT use cases have spurred its popularity, there is still a long way to go. The excitement surrounding the NFT has recently centered on the specialty fields of art, collectibles, and gaming. New NFT initiatives that merge on a regular basis, on the other hand, are gently but steadily expanding NFTs to various elements of our physical life.

Nike, for example, has patented its shoes as NFTs and dubbed them "CryptoKicks," which allow customers to crossbreed different sneakers to create a new unique sneaker. We'll probably see how NFTs develop to the point where they can be used in both physical and digital environments.

"How many game businesses will say, let's integrate those Nike sneakers within our digital games?" questioned Yat Siu, CEO of Animoca Brands.

As the value and promise that NFTs may give become clear to more people, a growing number of significant investors, huge brands and venture capital firms will become involved and pay attention.

According to reports, Morgan Creek Digital co-founders Jason Williams and Anthony Pompliano made a "huge bet" that digital art NFTs will outperform the physical art market.

We can also see that indie blockchain game creators have begun to attract venture capital because of their ability to provide flexible monetization methods and extremely extended product life cycles, making them perfect investments.

Governance tokens in the NFT industry are generating interest, much like they did for DeFi. It's impossible to predict what interesting new ways DeFi and NFTs will collide.

The NFT's future path may be difficult and fraught with regulatory obstacles. Regardless, the crypto field is still young and will continue to grow as a community with many more initiatives being developed, whether they succeed or fail.

Is the NFT phenomenon a bubble?

It's difficult to say. Music and art are difficult to value in and of themselves, and NFTs fall into this category. It could be a transient mania brought on by a collective emotional response to the pandemic. It might also be the beginning of a massive new virtual market segment.

For young risk-takers

In comparison to traditional markets, the NFT market has the potential to be more efficient. NFT is organized around online art markets.

When we look at the fees, we can see that they are less than 5% or even 10% of what typical art brokers charge. Every week, platforms such as OpenSea and Rarible count tens of thousands of unique wallet connections.

During the sector's tremendous expansion over the last five years, the first set of cryptocurrency holders has become millionaires. The crypto-wealthy generation is primarily made up of young risk-takers who can afford to experiment.

Despite the tremendous fluctuation of the price, research has shown that the public is becoming increasingly favorable to cryptocurrency adoption. Their willingness to take risks expands the crypto possibilities economy.

Although there are some highly promising uses for the technology in the gaming and luxury industries that will take 3 more years to become mature, some think that the frenzy for NFT, particularly in the art department, will be short-lived.

The audience of the NFT market is distinct from that of regular marketplaces. Banksy's heirs destroyed the artwork, and the WallStreetBets generation is betting against those massive hedge funds.

The NFT mania may be a passing fad. But, more crucially, it could signal a significant shift in the direction of the virtual economy. For better or worse, it is the first and primary disruptor.

Chapter 5. Platform to Sell NFT and its Requirement

After reviewing the prominent projects that employ NFTs and the relationship between NFTs and other types of art (photography, video makers, musicians and DJs), it's time to talk about the platforms that facilitate NFT trading.

A few of these venues were discussed in the previous, but their criteria and how to sell NFTs on them could be discussed in greater detail in this chapter.

Here is a list of platforms that make trading Non-Fungible Tokens simple (NTFs).

1. OpenSea: www.opensea.io

2. Rarible: www.rarible.com

3. SuperRare: www.superrare.com

4. Foundation: www.foundation.app

5. Atomic Market: www.wax.atomicmarket.io

6. Myth Market: www.myth.market

7. BakerySwap: www.bakeryswap.org

8. KnownOrigin: www.knownorigin.io

9. Enjin Marketplace: www.enjin.io/software/marketplace 10. Portion: www.portion.io 11. Async Art: www.async.art/

OpenSea

OpenSea promises to be the world's largest NFT marketplace.

Non-fungible tokens include antiques, sports, virtual worlds, trade cards, censorship-resistant web addresses, and art. ERC721 and ERC1155 characteristics are covered.

Axies, ENS titles, CryptoKitties, Decentraland, and other unique digital assets are accessible for purchase, sale and distribution.

There are around 700 projects to pick from, including collectible games and trading card games, naming systems, and interactive art projects like ENS (Ethereum Name Service).

Creators can use OpenSea's item minting tool to create blockchain-based objects. It allows you to create a set of NFTs by writing a line of code. You may connect to OpenSea by, for example, creating a smart contract for just an internet game or a digital asset on the blockchain.

You may sell products for a set price, a falling bid listing, or a cost listing on OpenSea.

Rarible

It is a society NFT (non-fungible token) platform that employs an ERC-20 RARI token as a type of ownership. Adjustable compensation for active users that purchase or trade on the NFT exchange with the RARI token. It delivers 75,000 RARI per week.

The website places a premium on art assets. Rarible allows developers to sell movies, art, CDs, music and books by "mining" new NFTs.

Visitors to Rarible can see a sample of the product, but only the customer has access to the whole project.

NFTs may be purchased and sold in a wide range of fields, spanning websites, music, athletics, metaverses, memes, photos, art, and many more.

SuperRare

SuperRare specializes in limited-edition and one-of-a-kind digital artworks. You can own and trade tokenized works of art generated by network artists. They define themselves as a cross between Christie's and Instagram, providing a new method for people to interact with collecting, culture and art on the internet.

Each work of art on SuperRare is a digital collectible, a blockchain-tracked digital item. SuperRare, in opposition to the market, has built a social network. Digital treasures are suited for a social context since they have a proven history of ownership.

In all transactions, the Ethereum network's native coin, Ether, is utilized.

You can fill out a form to submit your artist profile and have it evaluated for SuperRare's full launch in the future.

Foundation

It's a small group that brings together digital developers, crypto natives and fans to help grow the industry. The "new creative economy" has been coined. It focuses primarily on digital art.

It's a tiny club that pulls together electronic programmers, crypto natives and enthusiasts to assist the sector to thrive.

They suggested, "Hack, sabotage, and misuse the value of art."

In other words, when a collector actually sells their artwork to another person for a greater price, the artist earns 10% of the total sales.

AtomicMarket

It's a smart contract for the NFT market with mutual liquidity that's employed by a number of websites. Shared liquidity refers to the fact that whatever is available in one area appears in all others.

It is an EOSIO-based decentralized cryptocurrency for Atomic Properties, a non-fungible token protocol. It is feasible to establish a standard for tokenizing and producing digital assets for use on Atomic Assets marketplace.

Atomic- Market allows you to search for and list NFTs for sale. A verification check mark distinguishes genuine and well-known NFTs collections. Malicious collections are added to a blocklist.

Myth Market

It's a collection of user-friendly online marketplaces for a number of different digital trading card companies. KOGS, KOGS, KOGS, KOGS, KOGS, KOGS Pepe, go to the market. Heroes and the Market The market is where you may purchase digital Garbage Pail Kids cards.

This is one of the featured markets right now (for William Shatner memorabilia.)

BakerySwap

BakerySwap is an autonomous market maker (AMM) and decentralised exchange (DEX) that operates on the Alibaba Smart Chain (BSC). It makes use of the platform's own BakerySwap token (BAKE). It's a multi-purpose crypto hub that offers a variety of DeFi services, as well as an NFT marketplace and a crypto launchpad.

It accepts BAKE tokens for NFT, meme competitions and digital art.

BAKE tokens are obtained by combining NFTs. It is also simple to mint and sells.

KnownOrigin

KnownOrigin is a website where you can buy and sell exclusive digital artwork.

Each piece of digital art on KnownOrigin is one-of-a-kind. This platform allows artists to show and sell their work to collectors.

Ethereum blockchain is a project created by Ethereum.

The KnownOrigin gallery allows users to add jpeg or GIF files which is stored on IPFS

Enjin Marketplace

A blockchain property exploration and trading platform. Enjin-powered NFT marketplace. Enjin Coin has so far been used to buy 2.1 billion NFTs worth USD$43.8 million. There have been 832.7K transactions. The Enjin Wallet makes selling and buying gaming items simple.

For example, gamified reward systems in the Age of Rust, as well as the Six Dragons multiverses, include NFTs (such as Binance and Swissborg), Microsoft's Cloud Heroes, and community-created items.

Portion

This is a Blockchain-based electronic trading platform that enables collectors and artists to buy, trade, and invest in antiques and art in a fast and transparent manner. This endeavor is being supported by Artist Collaborative, a decentralized global network of content producers and artists.

Because of the portion, it's simple to gather. Cryptocurrency may be traded for antiques and art in one spot.

ERC-20 currencies can be used to work towards making decisions regarding the future of the blockchain. New tokens are given to potential and current team members. New Portion Tokens worth 500 PRT are given to artists who create new NFTs.

Async Art

Async Art is a blockchain-based artistic movement. It is necessary to form, collect, and share programmed art. "Masters" and "Layers" are available for purchase individually. Layers are the several components that make up the Final picture.

The artist determines the special skills of each layer. Any modifications made to a Layer will be visible to whoever owns the Master image. The limits of a designer are set by artist, and buyers have total control over all aspects of the piece. Users can alter the context, the location of a character, or the color of the sky, for example.

Chapter 6. How to Create NFTs

You probably think that NFTs are a great investment and that you'd like to purchase them. The previous chapters explained how NFTs function and some of the most common projects that they are used for.

Now is the moment to make a Non-Fungible Token. But, before we get started, let's go through some of the challenges that arise with NFTs.

Problems with the NFT

Despite its impact on numerous industries, non-fungible tokens are not without faults. Unfortunately, the source of your problems is blockchain.

Although decentralized networks aren't ideal, developers are tempted to improve them. Verifying the validity, selling, buying, and keeping an NFT, for example, all necessitate some understanding of Blockchain technology.

The issue arises because most individuals are only concerned with the product itself rather than the technology that underpins it.

When it comes to NFTS acceptance, Beeple, an NFT artist who sold a few of his works for USD$66,666 apiece, argues that "the basic infrastructure in place" ensures a positive experience for customers.

The terms "internet" and "smartphones" are interchangeable. Most people have no understanding of how these two works, but billions of people utilize them every day. We'll need the same experience in this scenario as we did with blockchain.

Creating your own NFT artwork in the form of a photograph or a GIF is a simple process that requires no crypto understanding. Collectibles and other digital card sets can be made with NFT.

But, before we get started, let's go through some of the challenges that arise with NFTs. Ethereum is the most extensively utilized blockchain platform for publishing NFTs.

Other blockchains, however, are gaining traction, including:

- WAX.
- Tron
- EOS
- Binance Smart Chain
- Tezos
- Polkadot
- Flow by Dapper Labs
- Cosmos

Each blockchain has its own standard NFT coin, as well as its own wallet and market services. One could only trade NFTs on websites that recognize Binance Smart Chain features if you utilize a Binance Smart Chain. That implies you can't sell it on an Ethereum-based system such as the VIV3 on the Flowing blockchain or OpenSea.

Connect your wallet to one of numerous NFT-centric services and upload the file or picture to be converted.

The following are Ethereum NFT marketplaces:

- Mintable
- OpenSea
- Rarible

NFTs may also be created on Makersplace, but you really should first register as just an artist.

A 'Create' button is available in Mintable, Rarible and OpenSea.

This is how OpenSea, the world's largest NFT market in Ethereum, works.

Click the blue "Create" button to add your Ethereum wallet.

The software links your wallet to the marketplace using your wallet password. You'll need a cryptographically signed letter in your Ethereum wallet to transmit money, but you may only click to verify your wallet address.

When you type your wallet password when prompted, the marketplace will automatically associate it with your wallet. Simply click to verify that your Ethereum wallet address is correct. The digital signature on communication is free of charge. This is only an instance to demonstrate how you can reach your financial goals.

The next stage on OpenSea would be to pick "My Collection" by hovering over "Generate" in the upper right corner. Then press the "Create" button in blue.

When you arrive at the window, you will be taken there, where you may name your item, describe it, and submit it.

To complete this step, just create a file for your freshly formed NFTs.

Once you've allocated a photo to your set, it will show (blue). Click the pen icon in the upper right corner to add a header picture (red).

The final product should look exactly like the one on the right.

You will now be the first one to create a new form of NFT. When you click the "Connect New Thing" button, your wallet will be used to sign a new communication (blue).

In a new window, your NFT artwork will appear.

Your NFT's rarity and uniqueness on OpenSea and other markets should be increased. Unlockable content may also be available from the creators, which can only be accessed by the purchaser. Passwords to online services, coupon codes and contact information are all instances.

On the Eth OpenSea platform, NFT capabilities are offered.

Once you're done, look at the bottom of a page and click "create" to sign another message to verify the NFT's existence in your wallet.

Creation cost of an NFT

For producing NFTs on OpenSea, certain platforms charge a fee. This charge is known as "gas" in Ethereum-based systems. The amount of Ether necessary to accomplish a blockchain function is referred to as ether gas. That will be the first time a new NFT is introduced to the market.

The price of gas varies due to network congestion. The price of gas rises as more people transfer value across the network. Here's a helpful hint: When transaction volume drops during the weekend, the cost of using Ethereum falls slightly.

This could lead to significant savings if you sell a lot of NFTs.

How to make and sell non-traditional digital art

Based on the NFT type, the configuration technique varies. You can utilize OpenSea, a well-known online seizure, to configure Digital NFTs Art.

Make a new wallet to hold Crypto and NFT. A meta mask wallet extension for Chrome is suggested by OpenSea.

Then, in the upper right corner of OpenSea, click on my profile.

To finish customizing your account, enter and then follow the screen prompts.

Then, in the upper right corner of your account, click on My Collections.

Then, click Create and fill in the details for a new collection.

When you choose to add a new device, you'll be prompted to offer your NFT a title and update its details.

Finally, click Create to complete the process.

When listing anything on OpenSea, sellers first must pay a gas price, which would be the Ether Blockchain transaction cost.

Rare and SuperRare are also excellent options. Today, one of the most prominent NTF markets is OpenSea. They can be used by artists to make money on the cryptocurrency market while also reaching out to new fans.

What can NFTs do?

NFTS may be used with DAPPs to build Digital collectibles and one-of-a-kind digital items. A billable item or an investment product.

The game of economics is not a new one. Aside from that, given how inexpensive many online games are already, blockchain adoption to tokenize gaming assets is a marvel. In reality, NFTs can help to decrease or eliminate the general inflation problem in a variety of games.

Another exciting application of NFT is the tokenization of real-world assets. This NFT will be used to symbolize a fraction of a real-world asset as a network token. Several markets that lack liquidity, such as rare collector items, property investment, art and many others, might benefit from this.

NFTs can benefit from digital specifications as well. Many individuals believe that putting identification and owning data on blockchain improves data confidentiality and authenticity. Global friction may be decreased by transferring assets in parallel, quickly, and consistently.

The story of Ethereum and CryptoKitties

Although CryptoKitties has been covered previously, its emergence is remarkable; so, it is worth emphasizing its connection to Ethereum.

Cryptokitties, an Ethereum-based system that will allow users to collect, nurture, and trade virtual kittens, was one of the first NFT enterprises to gain popularity.

Each CryptoKitty is one-of-a-kind in terms of color, breed and age. They're also not interchangeable. Because Cryptokitties tokens are indivisible, they cannot be divided (like the Ether for Gwei).

Due to high network activity, Cryptokitties sprang to notoriety as they jammed the block of blocks Ethereum. The popularity of Cryptokitties remains at an all-time high (ATH) for daily transactions on the Ethereum Blockchain.

Other events, such as the first feather currency offering, had an impact on the Ethereum network (ICO).

Other incidents have had an impact on the Ethereum network (ICO).

Blocks have been used for non-currency purposes since CryptoKitties.

They sold millions of dollars, with some rare artefacts bringing hundreds of thousands.

Detailed steps on how to create NFT art

Step 1: Create an artwork

Making your specialization is the most important thing to market NFT craftsmanship. This can include GIFs, visualizations, recordings, 3D models, and other media types. A brief stroll around Rarible or Foundation will provide you with an overview of the crypto art scene.

It seems that either extremely garde, innovative abstract art or catchphrase internet culture allusions are chosen at the moment.

Not that this should dictate your work; we're not going to go into an argument about "creating for the market" right now.

You can proceed to the following stage once you've determined what art you'd want to upload.

Step 2: Create Ethereum wallets.

There are several wallets to pick from to serve your visible address and store your private key; however, an equipment wallet is typically suggested.

Here's a quick crash course on how bitcoin wallets function if you're new to cryptocurrencies: They're essentially software or hardware that aid in managing the public address on your cryptocurrency blockchain.

Although its ownership is fully anonymous (until you make it otherwise), this public address contains the bitcoin, and anybody may access it.

Each public discourse is paired with a private key, which is used to bank, withdraw, or transmit payments to or from the address. It may be like a mailbox: everyone can see it, know where it is, and use it to send mail. Only those with the mailbox key may open it and retrieve the messages inside.

There are two sorts of wallets: those that give more ease, i.e., online pocketbooks at the sacrifice of security, and those that keep data offline, making them less convenient for widespread usage but substantially more secure.

Required to assist is a very well example of a wallet, while the greatest example of cold wallets are Trezor or Ledger hardware wallets, as well as pad of paper. Yes, you can construct a cold wallet out of paper and a pen, but you'll have to manufacture your public clothes, which might be uncomfortable.

Step 3: Buy ether

The fact that selling the NFT will cost you money may be news in the frenzy of information and increased interest in the NFT. Unlike Bitcoin miners, who are compensated in Bitcoin for contributing the processing power required to verify transactions and add entries to the blockchain, Ethereum miners are paid in gas, a different blockchain currency.

Each moment a payment is demanded to be made official and added to the blockchain, a transaction fee is paid (presumably to encompass the gas and platform fees) - Eth miners can choose which contracts to allot computational power to, so the more gas you pay for your payment, the faster it will be performed and added to the blockchain. Up-loading, your NFT, is one of them.

Step 4: Select a marketplace

When you have your piece, purse and some ether eating a hole in your pocket, you're prepared to sell your NFT.

Go to ethereum.org and read through their list of "Apps" (short for decentralized apps). Rarible, Nifty Gateway, and Foundation were excellent locations to begin learning about the Ethereum marketplace and observing your NFT.

Each and every one caters to somewhat different interests, so look into all three, as well as a range of other markets, before making a decision.

Nifty Gateway looks to be most adapted to digital art, Foundation seems to be better suited to 3D models, and Rarible appears to be a haphazard mash-up of garde and internet meme culture.

Step 5: Upload your artwork

While the location of the actual button changes depending on the concept, they always begin with linking your cryptocurrency wallet.

Each of the big sites will sign up for your that is linked to your wallet and will lead you through a very easy upload procedure in which you will be asked how so many "pieces" of a NFT you would like to mint and what percentage of royalties you want to get when the product is resold.

The latter component is game-changing for digital artists, who, unlike their conventional counterparts, have never been able to eventually limit the supply of a single piece once it has been circulated, resulting in a real "original."

The NFT contains a signed document written on the blockchain that validates that it is an original piece, allowing the original artist to earn from every subsequent trade/sale - a characteristic that even conventional artists will be unable to make use of. After you've selected your work, created your copies, and determined your royalties, you may go to the last stage.

Step 6: Pay the transaction fee

Once you've secured and published your NFT art, all you have to do now is pull a trigger and wait for your work of art to be transferred to the chain and changed into an exceptional substance on the organization, unchangeable and impervious to any worker crash.

Any Ethereum miner who acknowledges the arrangement and recovers your charge for their work will be able to mine your NFT thanks to the exchange fee.

After that, it should only take a few minutes for your newly mined NFT to hit the market, ready to please the eagle-eyed patron who notices it first.

Divided Opinion on NFTs

The digital resources market is increasing as a result of new financing approaches; nevertheless, the promise of collectible (in which digital tokens reflect title to real or virtual commodities) is the capacity for users to confirm their possession by generating unique digital money stored on the blockchain.

Unlike crypto assets, however, the community has voiced concerns about the true volume that NFTs would produce. However, in January of this year, monthly BTC futures trading volume exceeded $500 billion, and as of this write, NFT market trading activity has reached $8.2 million.

NFTs like digital paintings have failed to attract a large trading market. However, as the industry matures, it's feasible that more significant and more stable markets may emerge. Bringing in investors such as Paul Tudor Jones, Saylor and Musk is, of obviously, the same as considering them legendary in the bitcoin realm.

You should be able to deposit money on a blockchain and hold collateralized fiat-pegged stable currencies or borderless digital assets, among other things.

It is unknown if NFTs will profit while staying in the same flow stream as some other cryptocurrencies such as bitcoin and altcoins. Is it capable of making high-end auction houses and preserving high-net-worth collectors accessible to regular investors who spend tiny sums of money there?

Celebrities and NFTs

Lindsay Lohan's Twitter account has already begun to gain Bitcoin followers, while billionaire Mark Cuban eventually sold NFTs for $1,000 to buyers looking to sell his tweets as an NFT. Other celebrities will quickly follow suit, and it is only a question of time until more powerful people join the movement.

In other words, Ethernity is seeking to attract celebrities by offering digital artwork (including the above individuals) with each NFT transaction. The collection will be blessed by Paolo Maldini, Michael Rubin and the Winklevoss twins.

Michael Rubin is the originator of the All in Challenge, a charitable initiative that has earned more than $50 million for hunger-relief groups.

Ethernity was founded by Nick Rose Ntertsas. Per its website, it is a platform for celebrities, sports and artists from all over the globe to sell limited-edition artworks, with revenues benefiting the celebrity's selected charity. According to Rose, the painting they've bought is finished and ready to sell.

Hash marks is a recent success story in the use of NFTs. There is a venture where digital photos coexist with collectible NFTs, whose look is both desirable and greatly sought for. In just a few days, they've surpassed the $10 million ETH threshold.

In ETH, a one-of-a-kind and ultra-rare CryptoPunk NFT sold for $762,000. As the market valuation of digital art grows, it is predicted to exceed that of traditional art.

Growing

NFTs, according to Jehan, is the most critical missing connection between printed and electronic publications. NFTs are uncommon and transparent. This is because of the reason that they are entered into a public ledger, which safeguards precious items.

Some believe that NFTs will play an important role in the decentralized finance (Defi) industry. The Ethereum-based virtual world of Alpaca City provides proof of concept for this.

In under 15 minutes, Alpaca City's November token pre-sale garnered almost 1,000 ETH.

Owners of alpaca NFTs may "breed" them, changing the NFT market: NFT loans, attention accounts, and so on. Because NFT holders want to transfer and receive assets from many blockchains, interoperability is also essential.

Because of TRON's new NFT standard, TRC-721, which includes a defi primitive, tracing and transferring tokens is now feasible. All stakeholders, including those who support NFTs and those who oppose them, are coming to see the genuine value of NFTs.

Companies are providing safe and accessible NFT protocols, and buyers are rushing to get a piece of the action. Distributed Public Blockchain System Decentraland, Hashmasks and CryptoPunks are using Ethereum to begin NFT operations.

Virtual reality is a universe that resembles a digital land in which people may interact with one another, explore, buy land plots, and even start new enterprises.

Next Move?

Investor interests, the expansion and profitability of the VR/AR gaming business, and the advent of NFT-specific blockchains to power ecosystems will all play a role.

Finally, assuming constant gas prices, estimating the NFT market potential is difficult (particularly Ethereum) because novel finance methods have yet to establish their potential to retain wealth through time, substantial concerns persist.

NFTs have less liquidity than more liquid financial products (but growing). Obtaining one is straightforward; however, finding a willing buyer who shares your interests is more challenging.

People aren't thrilled with uninvited NFTs at the finish of a song when they can't play anymore. And the celebration is presently in full swing. On February 8, a buyer paid $1.5 million for nine distinct NFT plots. This transaction set a new NFT record as well.

In terms of price, digital real estate has now officially eclipsed traditional real estate. It might be hysteria, but a rising number of crypto-savvy investors are jumping on the bandwagon.

Digitalizes have realized that selling anything on the Internet may increase the public's collective power. Despite the fact that humanity is connected, tokenization is very likely in the near future.

Selling an NFT

Because a simple rule will work across all platforms, it's a smart idea to start there.

Organizing your wallet Since you may use cryptocurrencies and non-fungible tokens (NFTs), you must first save them in a virtual wallet.

We suggest that you use Chrome Browser and download the MetaMask wallet plugin more to safeguard your transfers. Look up MetaMask's commonly asked questions and suggestions on this site. After installing OpenSea, go over to the upper right side, click on the icon, and then select My Login. After you receive your wallet, you will receive instructions for login in.

Creating a collection

We are indeed developing on a website in which you can check your account balance, but it should be up and running shortly. Select My Favorites from the drop-down bar, then click the Add button on the top-right side.

Once you've completed assembling your collection, give it a name and a short description, as well as a photo; we're not yet developing an NFT, so you'll be free to change all of this information once you've finished. By using Add New Items option will take you behind the operations and show you the full breadth of your library.

Fine-tuning your collection

Although getting going on your very first NFTs is crucial, there are some things you must do initially. Above, you can see a personalized banner to the right of the image. Click the "Make Your Personal" pencil symbol in the upper right-hand corner to upload your own design. Aim for a resolution of 1400x400 pixels and avoid using text. On the Purchases tab, you'll notice pending additional sales transactions (which will now be held in your bank account) and selecting Visit will take you to the public library.

To add social links photos and edit the item's title, description and image, go to "Edit." Additionally, if you leave the Accepted Payment Tokens option alone, you will be able to increase the resale tax to 10%. If you really want 5% of the total sales value for your NFTs, go to the "Earn a Part of Future Sales" page and enter 5 in the "Profit to Recipients" box. Then go to the "Sellers Address" tab and type in your wallet address there. When you're done, click the Make Changes button to be taken to your company's back office.

Announcement of items for sale

Going to a publicly visible property page and selecting "Sell" is the simplest way to submit your NFT. Choose a fixed-price advertisement over a price-based auction. If you're in a positive mood, adhere to the guidelines in your wallet and then click Submit your ad.

If you've never sold it before, you'll have to pay a gas tax before you can offer it on OpenSea. The deal should be straightforward once the Ethereum network gets less busy.

You'll also be asked to validate the token in a currency other than ETH, which will result in a different (but cheaper) gas cost. Consequently, you will not have to pay anything again.

You'll be required to validate your WETH and pay a gas cost before you can make a bid for a listed item if you use WETH. Buyers of fixed-price properties must pay a gas fee. When it comes to selling, sellers pay when they accept bids.

Don't be concerned that the procedure will take a long time because there are so many other persons involved. When you return to the posting procedure, our framework will recognize that your wallet has completed the exchange and will not urge you to pay fees when you create the next posting.

Projects build a strong foundation under the DEFI and NFTS marriage

The Meet team has made the NFT market almost as complicated, adaptable, and liquid as the rest of the Crypto market.

The digital collection on Blockchains is driving a retail frenzy for greater Crypto today, partly because they're cool and partly because the market appears to have finally reached this consensus: the possession of digital commodities that can be confirmed has actual value.

If there is genuine ability, there is profits to be saved. In the latest days, this class of tokens, also known as non-fungible (NFTS) tokens, has been shown to have an incredibly high value.

A new service for NFTFI is now being developed as a data point in the sequence of NFT-Decentralization Financial unions. Borrowers use this tech to add digital things to their credit reports as collateral. Those that contributed to the $ 890,000 round included RoehhamGhehamlou, Dapper Labs Coinfund, Lao,1kx and others. The investment was disclosed by NFTFI on Thursday.

NFTFI is one of numerous companies that collaborate with third-party suppliers to find things simpler to accept funds, obtain results, and recover money back from the virtual collecting room.

How does it work?

Ave and Defi Giants Compounding are financial sectors, but they operate on the basis of exchangeable guarantees, such as different traditional currencies or ET. NFT is not practical since these marketplaces lack liquidity, making it more difficult to identify prices.

If more products are introduced to the market, the market changes faster, making it easier for liquidity to circulate through with a greater number of producers. Remember, this is Crypto: rapid development means completely different things in our business than it did in the days of virtual communities and Pokey devices, which is fantastic.

"NFTs begin to construct new financial advisory types when they predict how we produce and recognize digital information's ownership online," says MitraLasse Clausen, a partner at 1kx venture capital company.

The 10 initiatives listed below, which are not linked with NFTFI, work in roughly identical ways to confuse, adapt, and liquidate the NFT marketplace, as well as the remainder of the Crypto space:

Nintex.

The platform, a startup, is working on a new edition with a slew of new features. The government's authority over the underpinning NFT benefits holders of tools and portions that permit for more flexible ownership. The app will likewise be managed by a DAO.

"This is self-evident. One-of-a-kindness reigns supreme, "In an email to Coindesk, Joel Hubert said.

Ark Gallery.

NFT pioneer lava labs become more fungible as a result. Ark then set up additional measures to boost liquidity for original non-fungible tokens, which may be credited with the current cryptopunks craze. In an email to Coindesk, Roberto Ceria Ark said, "We will launch the NFT project."

Metabase.

Mintbase enables creating non-fungible tokens simply. It just completed a fundraising round led by the Chinese. Sales royalties can be dispersed to up to 1,000 people using the Mint base. "It's actually a part of the fractional ownership discussion," COO CAROLIN told Coindesk.

NFTX

This enables public index funds to own a large number of NFTs with just one token. It has tokens for several NFT categories as well as the market spectrum. "Many consumers want market exposure but lack the skills or time to trade individual NFTs.

Defi

In the crypto ecosystem, a hot new movement is gaining traction: defi. Although Defi is not precisely new, the success of the YFI crypto token has piqued traders' and investors' interest in Defi and its connected cryptocurrencies.

Even if you just trade the larger cryptocurrencies like Bitcoin and Ethereum, the Defi boom should be monitored since it may have an impact on your assets. Here's a quick rundown of what's going on at Defi, YFI and the crypto market as a whole.

Nice increase at YFI

Cryptocurrency prices have been in a stronger position, as cryptocurrency outperformed everyone else by rising 165 percent to $ 38,682. This is YFI, the governing token for the millennial Financing network's decentralized finance (Defi).

Through the Defi logs, Yearn aggregates the various yields. Users earn money by lending their coins to different protocols or keeping them in "vaults." Users that contribute liquidity for the practice known as "yield farming" can also acquire governance tokens like YFI. As the name indicates, owners of these administration coins can vote on system ideas.

YFI-like coins got on the Defi bandwagon and saw their prices rise as well. YF Link's price increased by 328 percent to $ 581, YFFI's to $ 84.14 (465 percent), and YFV's to $ 56.62. (201 percent). In three days, YFII, a subsidiary of YFI, soared from $ 935 to $ 5,076.

Administration coins are becoming a hot speculative investment since the supply is limited, and investors wish to get in before it's too late. The number of YFI tokens available is restricted to 30,000, with 29,962 currently in circulation, because these tokens are very liquid, a single large transaction may have a tremendous influence on the market; one of the reasons for such dramatic price changes is that they are highly liquid.

Invest in Defi

Everyone appears to want to get into Defi, but what exactly does this phrase imply? Defi stands for "Decentralized Finance," and it tries to duplicate the application areas of our old financial system using high-tech, little bureaucracy and no middlemen.

This implies that instead of banks, a decentralized open-source network is used to issue and borrow money, trade derivatives and securities, take out insurance, invest, and so on. Smart contracts, which are verified by blockchain participants, automatically carry out the conditions of financial agreements. The current market capitalization of Defi smart contracts is over USD$8 billion.

Defi and Ethereum

Anyone interested in Ethereum should recognize this. In reality, Ethereum is used by the great majority of these applications. Other networks with cryptographic protocol capability should be compatible with Defi, while Ethereum is currently the market leader. The popularity of DeFi should theoretically help ETH as well.

Yearn Finance's main products are "safes," which provide the greatest returns to yield farmers while pooling funds to lessen customers' effort. As per the cryptocurrency world, Yearn's ETH bunkers are projected to increase interest for ETH while lowering supply as more Ethereum coins are locked in the vault for yield farming.

Boom or bubble?

While some investors are eager to seize the opportunity of high profits that yield farming offers, following the newest trend is not always the best course of action. The 2017-2018 ICO boom will be remembered fondly by long-time crypto aficionados. Many Defi ventures are still in the early stages of development and carry both risks and rewards.

Industry executives have also attacked yield farming, which is truly fueling the Defi rush. When it comes to Defi, Ethereum co-founder VitalikButerin has cautioned investors. He compares the yield farming business model to the Federal Reserve's printing (which causes inflation in the number of governance tokens).

Invest in the crypto future with StormGain

As is customary for a skilled trader, he will conduct research on certain investments. However, after the dust has cleared on the Defi boom, cryptocurrency will triumph across the board as the blockchain's applications become more evident.

As a result, we advocate building a varied and flexible crypto portfolio on a platform that pays you well for your involvement.

Stormgain is the market's most effective bitcoin trading platform. Stormgain is an easy-to-use platform that allows you to trade the top six altcoins with up to 200x margin around the clock through the Web or a mobile application. Stormgain also has the finest client benefits on the market, including yearly interest rates of up to 15% on cryptocurrency deposits.

How does Auctioning work in the marketplace?

NFTs are part of a $250 million sector that is rapidly increasing. The market for non-fungible tokens, or NFTs, has increased to $250 million, according to a 2020 research by L'Atelier BNP Paribas. Investments in NFTs increased by 299 percent in 2020, as cryptocurrencies such as Bitcoin grew in popularity.

Millions were made by NFT producers and resellers. After investing $67,000 on the Beeple project, an art dealer made $6.6 million on a 10-second digital artwork.

NFTs include digital trade activities, virtual property investment, art and cards. Here's how you can begin purchasing and trading NFTs. Unlike popular cryptocurrencies such as Bitcoin and Ether, NFTs cannot be exchanged and distributed directly across multiple platforms.

Most NFT platforms enable purchasers to utilize Flow, WAX or Ethereum with a digital wallet.

Artists and merchants have made millions of dollars from visual art.

Mike Winkelmann's "Crossroads" was resold on Nifty Portal for USD$6.6 billion. Artists can get royalties on the majority of digital-art trade sites.

Some cater to a small group of people, while others invite anybody to make and sell their art.

Professional digital artists received a windfall of benefits as a result of NFTs. Visual arts trade systems, as according to NFT designer Trevor Jones, may obviate the need for more traditional art exchanges. NFTs have piqued the curiosity of several conventional marketplaces.

In February, Christie's, the auction house founded in 1766, auctioned a Beeple piece, marking the first step into digital tokens. With two days till the auction concludes, the painting is currently valued at $9.75 million.

Platforms like Nifty Gateway, Foundation and SuperRare, which let buyers pick from a carefully chosen range of work, include the work of multimillion-dollar digital artists.

It's fantastic since Nifty Gateway lets artists who previously exclusively shared their work on Instagram and Twitter do so. They began selling crypto art after the advent of crypto money and are now reaping the advantages and rising recognition.

Virtual comic artists Chris Torres and Grimes have found homes on sites such as Nifty Portal, SuperRare and Foundations. Artists get paid a license of around 10% of any potential sales of their work via these sites.

Although the usage of credit cards by purchasers makes Nifty Gateway's site more accessible to buyers, other platforms place a greater focus on lowering the entry barrier for developers.

Unlike Zora and Rarible, which are invitation-only sites, Mintable and Rarible let anyone publish, trade, and trade images and text as non-traditional products.

On these sites, artists can still receive royalties, but the material is less tightly supervised than on the other pages. Rarible users can contribute anything, from blank images to their own interpretations of well-known works of art.

Robert Martin, a Rarible NFT engineer, says the sites' security has to be improved, but he compliments the simplicity with which users may post information to Rarible.

These websites sell NFTs for a range of costs, from $10 to hundreds of thousands of dollars.

NFT and sports

NBA Top Shot sells sports videos for a range of rates, ranging from $20 to thousands of dollars.

Fantasy sports' popularity has also had an influence on NFT earnings. Users may build, sell, and manage virtual teams utilizing digital player cards using a unique fantasy soccer platform.

This website was only recently founded in 2018, and it has only recently begun to gain popularity among users. Sorare recently sold about USD$13 million in ether, according to the cryptocurrency news site CryptoSlam.

Gamers and trading-card collectors

Axie Infinity manufactures NFTs for the gaming industry. Axie Infinity manufactures NFTs for the gaming industry. Axie developed the imaginary character Axie Infinity.

According to CryptoSlam, Axie Infinity, a firm that sells cartoon animals that battle like Pokémon, is one of the top ten most popular crypto-collecting websites on the Internet.

Non-traditional gameplay is anticipated to become more successful. Altitude Games' Combat Racers, a cryptocurrency racing game, has been released on the Arkane Market, which has over 100,000 players.

Another well-known trading card and memorabilia website are Myth. Two of my favorite locations in the world are Market and Treasureland. NFT gaming is predicted to continue to flourish.

Virtual real estate market

On Decentraland, users may purchase and trade digital property. Janine Yorio, the co-founder of Republic Real Estate, believes that digital real estate will emerge as Decentraland's next big investment industry.

Decentraland, a non-fungible coin (NFT) platform owned and administered by people and founded on the Ethereum blockchain, mixes VR technology and real estate on the Ethereum blockchain. It's a role-playing multiplayer game that allows people to create a virtual universe in a networked first-person shooter (NFT). The game resembles a more complex version of "SimCity," "Minecraft," or "Fortnite," according to Yorio.

According to reports, Atari, the company behind Pacman, wants to launch a bitcoin casino on this platform.

The price of the network currency "MANA" has risen by more than 321 percent in the last year, having a market worth of $225 million.

According to Twitter CEO Jack Dorsey, the site's very first tweet is auctioned out as a non-monetary transaction (NFT). Depending on its market value, the digital asset is currently worth 2.5 million dollars. Valuables is a website that allows users to swap their tweets for ether, a cryptocurrency.

The website's main purpose is to sell tweets in the form of NFTs. Glass Factory is another popular platform.

You may make digital art such as holograms and sell them as tokens on the secondary market.

Peter Redwall, an artist, sold his personal information to NFT, which included his social media profiles, weight and date of birth.

Chapter 7. NFT Lending & Borrowing

Lending with Fungible assets Vs. Non-fungible ones

During the last two years, crypto lending platforms have grown at an exponential rate. When people were questioning what the future of the utility of space would be in 2018, we can now see that lending is playing a key part in giving real value in the markets for products that have actual traction and adoption.

It's normal for collectors to want to leverage their NFT assets without selling them as the market grows, and the need can be even greater when you consider the underlying values.

When we compare lending with non-fungible and fungible assets, however, there are a few key differences:

1. Valuation is done automatically and precisely with fungible lending. The marketplace also sets the price realistically. While most projects in the NFT field face a significant barrier because the price is largely determined by scarcity rather than volume. As a result, the assessment may be subjective.

2. If we look at the fungible assets lending platforms, we can see that they exclusively deal with a few high-liquidity assets. However, in the NFT arena, this is nearly impossible due to the large number of projects available, as well as the fact that the attributes of each asset vary greatly within each project. It is their distinct quality that distinguishes them.

3. In the case of fungible lending, liquidation occurs automatically as borrowing prices approach market values and the LTV ratio reaches a certain level. Platforms and creditors will not suffer because of this technique. However, because the NFT market is

driven by scarcity, we cannot have thresholds for verifying the entire project and the category of assets' actual volume associated with the collateral assets inside the game because the NFT market will always have downtime or friction in the situation of the system automatically liquidating the assets to cover the lenders' loss.

We can observe that NFT lending has certain distinct issues compared to traditional crypto lending with fungible assets if we comprehend and evaluate these factors. But it's not all bad news.

Why do we need NFT debt markets?

The debt market is a significant missing piece in the NFT ecosystem. People must be able to borrow money from or sell their NFTs.

Many NFT users keep their funds in their wallets and don't utilize them unless they connect with the platform or play a specific game. Their NFTs accumulate dust in the wallet because they're not in demand.

It would be fantastic if people had options to rent their assets or use them as security for loans. It also benefits other users who require NFTs at the time.

How do the NFT collateralize loans work?

Let's take a look at how the NFTfi platform works to better understand the process. NFT is a simple marketplace for non-financial-to-financial-to-financial-to-financial-to.

For Borrowers:

Make use of your NFTs as collateral. Borrowers can use any ERC-721 token to secure a loan. Other users may be willing to lend them money. If the borrowers accept the loan, the ETH is sent from the lenders' account to the borrowers' account, and the NFT is locked in the NFTfi smart contract.

When they repay the loans, the resources will be returned to them. Their assets will be transferred to the lender if they do not repay the entire loan amount by the due date.

For Lenders:

Get enticing returns. Lenders can search their favorite NFTs, such as Decentraland and crypto kitties, for loans on assets they're willing to lend on. Then, along with the loan amount, term and repayment amounts, submit the proposal. In the worst-case scenario, the borrowers are unable to pay, and the asset is forfeited.

Small, short-term loans to others can also reward them with good profits. They must, however, be knowledgeable about the NFT assets they are supplying and willing to accept the collateral if the lender defaults.

NFT valuation questions

This is a fascinating section. Let's imagine a CryptoKitty was previously sold for 30 ETH. Is it still worth 30 ETH? Etherscan can assist you in this. We can see what this kitty's last sale price was.

However, determining the value of an NFT based on its past sale price is simple but inaccurate. A similar examination of the valuation in terms of the kitty's species, qualities and the CryptoKitties market trend as a whole is required.

To appropriately evaluate the CryptoKitties, we'll need either detailed knowledge of the CryptoKitties or a request for advice from a prominent community member. Leaving it to the markets may be the most cost-effective price method.

An NFT valuation solutions

The NFT Collateralized Loan Marketplace could be a useful tool for determining the fair value of NFTs. Users can post their NFTs as collateral on these marketplaces, and others can bid on how much they are willing to lend against them.

The length of the loan term and whether the lender accepts DAI or ETH should also be options. It may be possible to produce a fair valuation of NFTs as a result of this.

For example, after doing my own research, I am willing to contribute 10 ETH for a five-month period. However, another CryptoKitties specialist recognizes that this is a one-of-a-kind opportunity and is willing to offer 15 ETH for five months.

Multiple offers and appraisals can aid in the creation of a much more accurate appraisal. It can be inefficient at first, but it can eventually lead to more stable NFT valuations.

NFT lease

In the markets, there might be an NFT leasing section where consumers can look at different NFTs that are offered to lease. The lessee can provide the number of NFTs for which they are willing to lease them, and the lessee can specify the number of NFTs for which the lessee wants to lease the asset. It would be beneficial to the markets if both sides were willing to customize their products.

If the market can predict user behavior, it can focus on popular categories such as "lend for one month" or "lend for one week." Predefined and restricted loan categories can make it easier for new users to understand the leasing market and help it expand beyond its initial user base. This will provide NFT owners with even another money stream.

When NFTs become widespread, the NFT leasing industry will be enormous. This is not only because people enjoy trying new things and playing new games but also because they will want to maximize the value of their possessions by leasing or lending them out.

How to value NFTs for lease

The NFT leasing market, like the NFT loan market, can assist in fairly valuing NFTs: the leasing market can assist in determining a fair leasing value for NFTs. Due to the nature of the assets, it may be more reliant on NFT types in the leasing market.#

If you're breeding assets like Axie or Crypt toKitties, for example. They can't always be efficiently bred. If the bred Axie or kitten has specific breeding properties, the lease value for breeding operations can be very high.

On the other side, if you need to mine Crypto Space Commanders resources quickly, you can rent a spaceship exclusively for mining and then return it after the resources have been gathered.

This type of requirement is likely to be uncommon, the market would theoretically price this asset for leasing at a low cost.

There seem to be various factors to consider before determining the market value of NFT leasing. Marketplaces, on the other hand, can assist in determining appropriate prices for these activities.

Current state

NFT, Starter, Lendroid and UniLend are some of the current options that allow NFT owners to borrow money by using their NFTs as collateral.

However, the majority of them are still in their infancy. The Starter and NFTfi were the two who went the furthest among them. The

Rinkeby version is available on Starter, while NFTfi is the only one on the mainnet.

So yet, no alternative systems that actively work on NFT-based lending appear to exist. Here are two initiatives worth mentioning:

A project called "Rocket" attracted a lot of attention around the start of 2020.

Alex Masmej is the one who starts it. Unfortunately, it has not yet been released to production since I was writing the book. The team also intends to hand over ownership of the project to the highest bidder.

Dragos I. Musan had another early-stage notion. Dragos presented theoretical methods for bridging some of the current gaps in NFT markets by employing appropriate Defi principles. However, only proof-of-concept solutions based on his described concepts have been built thus far, and they have similar functionality to NFTfi.

Future of NFT Lending

Unleashing the Defi application potential in the NFT domain is likely to result in a significant rise in market useability and activity. Users can earn a passive income via NFT loan and lease marketplaces, as well as a more accurate assessment of these NFT assets.

We're living in the Friendster age of NFTs. However, by using the regular crypto market and adapting it for NFTs, we are coming closer to the MySpace era.

We can expect a Facebook era with a seamless user experience as NFTs reach millions of users and the highly liquid and robust marketplaces. The initial phase will be to continue developing and implementing classic crypto ecosystem use-cases for the NFT ecosystem.

NFT Royalties

Because the majority of NFTs are produced as ERC-721 tokens, that will be the case after an artist sells their work to a buyer for the first time. It is the only time they are paid for their efforts if the buyer decides to sell it.

The source of information was then resold for 10 times its original price on the secondary market. None of this is visible to the final artist.

Many platforms have recognized this problem and are working to address it.

Attempting to improve the situation Let's have a look at two different platforms.

OpenSea

Users of Opensea can now profit from secondary sales of things. When a piece is sold on OpenSea, the project owner can earn a percentage of the sale as extra money.

This not only allows producers to profit from the sale of their initial work to consumers, but it also allows them to profit as their game and marketplaces grow in popularity.

To set up the secondary sale charge, creators simply go to their storefront editor. The earnings will be transferred every two weeks to the creators' selected payment address. They can also modify the frequency by contacting OpenSea.

Zora

This is yet another new NFT platform that allows developers of NFTs to establish a "creator share," or the proportion of future sales that they will get if they set the creator share at 20%, for example.

If the initial piece was sold for 1 ETH and then subsequently sold for 10 ETH, the author would be paid an additional 2 ETH for the secondary sale. The inventor never needs to worry over finding these developer shares because they are distributed periodically via smart contracts and are auditable on Ethereum.

They will just be compensated in perpetuity to their initial Ethereum addresses for launching the NFT.

You may have noticed a difficulty up until now: the mechanisms used by these platforms to pay creator shares are currently not replicable on the secondary market. The creator share percentages are only paid out if the second sale occurs on the same platform as the original sale, which is either OpenSea or Zora.

To create the ERC-721 Royalty standard, James Morgan and Zach Burks wrote an "Ethereum Improvement Proposal" (EPI-2981). The fundamental aim for this is to create a modified NFT standard that ensures that NFTs manufactured, bought, or sold on one marketplace continue to pay royalties regardless of whatever market they are sold on next.

This standard allowed creators to control the number of royalties paid to them on any marketplace that uses these tokens.

Let's return to the Zora example with this thought in mind. If the NFT was made on Zora, the artists would be entitled to a creator share if the customers sold it on another platform.

We could witness another surge in the NFT ecosystem if more merchants begin to adopt this standard.

Recur, an NFT platform raised $5 million in March 2021 for everlasting cross-platform NFT royalties, which is a promising step toward universal NFT royalties.

Their key innovation, in comparison to the two platforms listed above, is an ERC token standard that allows royalties to function regardless of platform.

"Our team is working on Ethereum upgrades, and our technology will be deployed at the blockchain layer," stated Recur Co-CEO Zach Bruch. "Through this novel technique, NFT generated on RECUR's platform will be able to travel freely throughout the environment while still producing recurring royalties for the network's owners and IP holders."

The eventual purpose of RECUR is to make NFTs chain agnostic and decentralize NFTs and royalties."

An interesting example in Music Industry

Treum, a ConsenSys Mesh portfolio business, recently released EulerBeats, a collection of 27 algorithmically generated music and art NFTs. When the number of prints in circulation for a particular original increase, the price of the next print issue increases exponentially.

ERC-1155, a modified version of ERC-721, was utilized. It means that the original LP holder will receive an 8% royalty on all future sales, while Treum will receive a 2% royalty. After two weeks, the smart contract governing the specific LPs paid directly out 912 ETH ($1,429,012 equivalent) in royalties.

The music metadata is included in the token implementation for other NFTs whose metadata is hosted on the centralized web server. This is important because even if the EulerBeats website went down, the beat and art generation scripts saved on the Ethereum blockchain might continue to operate indefinitely.

We may store a verifiable, one-of-a-kind audio piece on ETH, and future sales will be paid out to the original owners immediately. This might usher in a new way of marketing music.

It sounds interesting. In 2021, enterprising artists will begin to digitize audio recordings and sell them straight to their audience as NFTs. Simultaneously, a universal NFT royalty standard is being developed. Therefore, a new concern arises: how does all of this interact with established executing rights organizations?

The short answer is that what occurs on ETH continues to exist in its environment. The Mechanical Licensing Collective (MLC) chose ConsenSys and Harry Fox Agency last year to modernize music royalties payment and data in the coming years.

ConsenSys launched the MLC bridge in January, and it is continually improving. The MLC platform presently contains more than 48 million tracks and 9,400 music publishers. In addition, they recently received $424 million in overdue royalties.

We will see a convergence of both worlds in the near future as more PROs and music publishers become comfortable with the benefits provided by NFTs.

Before then, if you're an artist who's dissatisfied with the current royalties system, it's worth looking at what other musicians are up to in the NFT ecosystem.

Chapter 8. Other Options to Get Exposures to NFTs

"What is the greatest approach to get exposure to NFT markets?" is a question that is frequently tweeted and commented on under NFT-related posts as the NFT gain bull run continues.

It's nearly impossible for every NFT investor to devote hours each day to learning about the NFT ecosystem. The subject of how to obtain exposure to NFT in the first place is still being debated.

Another of the drawbacks of NFTs is that they are not publicly traded, liquid coins that can be purchased when the hype train comes. You undoubtedly learned from the previous chapters that

NFTs are extremely diversified, have many factors driving their values, and are thinly traded. Newcomers cannot simply hop in and begin purchasing. Actually, they could, but they'll probably regret it later because the vast majority of NFTs are worthless.

So, how can you obtain exposure to NFT as an investor if you aren't in the NFT ecosystem 24 hours a day, 7 days a week? Let's have a look at some additional possibilities.

Options #1 – Ethereum (ETH)

ETH is currently used to price 99 percent of NFT marketplaces. Other cryptocurrencies are growing in popularity as payment options, but ETH is possibly the most commonly used. Users will check the ETH price instead of the USD equivalent to make their NFT purchasing and selling decisions.

Assume you purchased an NFT for 1 ETH when the price of ETH was $1500.

They're now looking to sell that NFT for 1.2 ETH. If the value of ETH fell to $1000, the NFT would only be worth $1200 in comparison. Will you have the ability to sell it right away?

Most NFT market participants would like to take the profit from ETH since they are long-term bullish on the currency, and they would most likely reinvest that ETH into new NFTs.

Although this isn't always the case, I've noticed that the bulk of NFT participants is attempting to obtain additional ETH.

Investing in ETH is a straightforward way to gain light exposure to NFT markets because every NFT market participant utilizes ETH, and the majority of them reinvest their ETH into more NFTs.

Block is a cryptocurrency exchange where you can buy, trade, and exchange a variety of cryptocurrencies, including ETH, for low prices. You can also start earning up to 8.6% APY as soon as you place your deal. Your earnings will be compounded daily, and you will be paid monthly.

Options #2 -$RARI

Another interesting way to gain exposure to NFTs is to invest in the $RARI token, which allows users to receive it for NFT trading. Rarible is a large NFT exchange platform, and $RARI is its governance token, as we learned.

People were instantly enticed to start trading NFTs because they could earn $RARI by doing so. Users will not only receive a token for their NFT trades, but they will also gain control over the Rarible platform. As it is a governing currency, you may use it to recommend and vote on new projects on the Rarible network. Having a token that can affect the decisions of the major NFT exchanges appears to be a good way to obtain NFT exposure.

$RARI is not a formal investment vehicle; rather, it is earned by active engagement on Rarible. Each week, 75,000 tokens are issued, with 50% reserved for vendors and 50% reserved for buyers.

Following are the groups of people eligible to participate in the airdrop, according to Rarible:

Existing Rarible users: Based on the Liquidity Mining principle, which is determined by the prior volume on Rarible, active users can obtain 2% of the entire RARI supply.

Buyers and holders of NFTs are listed below: 4% of all NFTs with verifiable sales on Dune Analytics will be distributed to ETH addresses.

Owners of remaining NFTs: Rarible is aware that Dune Analytics may not have all of the data; thus, this is a workaround. If you are not able to position yourself on the list but are aware that you have major NFT holds, you can contact them for assistance.

Option #3 $WHALE

This is a more straightforward method of connecting to NFTs.

WhaleShark, a large NFT collector, produced $WHALE as a social token. It's supported by the value of the NFTs in "The Vault," which is a 3,500-strong NFT collection that WhaleShark recently bought. As a $WHALE owner, you can spend it to purchase things from the vault, such as virtual land, art, gaming components, and more.

Nonfungible.com, an NFT data source, also provides monthly vault audits. The WhaleShark now controls the vault where NFTs can be purchased, but the entire $WHALE ecosystem is moving to a DAO structure that serves as a decision-making vehicle.

Option #4 Flamingo DAO

Flamingo DAO is a fascinating NFT project created by the same people who founded the successful DAO venture fund LAO.

It's a for-profit DAO that's solely focused on the NFT ecosystem. Flamingo invests directly in NFTs, utilizes them as collateral for lending, fractionalizes NFTs, and so has a thorough understanding of the entire NFT ecosystem.

One factor that may deter people from joining is the steep minimum membership fee of 60 ETH. They also require accredited US investors.

Option #5 – NFT Bundles

The Nifty Onez NFT bundles created by GrowYourBase are one of the finest ways for the most of investors to obtain exposure to NFTs.

These bundles are amazing since they were designed by GrowYourBase, which means they're jam-packed with fantastic NFTs.

GrowYourBase has a lot of experience with NFTs and knows which ones to include in their bundles.

It's also an earn-and-learn site, with information on various NFTs as well as opportunities to earn NFTs.

Many NFTs in the Onez bundles can be fractionalized using NIFTEX, another NFT fractionation platform. These fractions are referred to as "shards," and they allow users to acquire NFT pieces.

A $1,000,000 Banksy, for example, is beyond of reach for most people. The owner, on the other hand, can fractionalize it on NIFTEX, and purchasers can buy shards of it, allowing them to possess a portion of it.

On NIFTEX, there are two popular Onez bundles:

The Onez Bundle is a one of the best ways to store money. It's an art-focused package including artwork from 20 top crypto artists, including Goldwell, Josie, Lucho Poletti and Pranksy.

Meta Onez Virtual Land Bundle: This bundle concentrated on virtual land rather than art. It has two Decentraland parcels, two Somnium Space parcels, twenty-one Sandbox parcels, and five Cryptovoxel parcels.

These two bundles are also visible on Dapp Radar's shardmarketcap.io website.

These two options may be suitable for anyone who wants to learn more about NFTs and the various industries within the NFT ecosystem.

Try a couple of Nifty ONEz shards if you're not sure which artists are hot.

Try some Meta ONEz shards if you're not sure which virtual land exchange is ideal.

This is an effective approach for the public to obtain NFT exposure without spending an inordinate amount of time researching the NFT ecosystem, as long as the curators designing these bundles know what they're doing.

Chapter 9. FAQs Related to NFTs

This chapter will answer some important questions concerning NFTs.

Some of the subjects presented in this section of the Q&A have previously been covered in prior chapters; nonetheless, a review helps to tie everything together.

How do NFTs work?

These may be produced using non-fungible coins and Blockchain contracts. The first widely utilized blockchains were NEO, EOS, and Ethereum. NFT-tokens are a unique crypto property that may be used to signify both tangible and immaterial objects.

Real things, such as buildings, electronics and other real objects, can be touched, but immaterial products can only be sensed indirectly. The ability of an asset to be traded for the same items, such as gold or dollars, is referred to as fungibility.

For art, for example, non-fungibility is an irreplaceable or unique asset capability.

The blockchain is digital evidence of authenticity and trustworthiness that uses non-fungible coins. It saves a record of your transactions.

NFT creates a creative platform for undervalued things and makes it simple for collectors to amass art online. NFTs (non-fungible tokens) have developed over time as the sector has grown. Beeple is a well-known brand name in the area of NFTs.

NFTS can be developed and distributed in a number of different ways. ERC-721 is a standard for publishing and exchanging non-fungible assets on the Ethereum blockchain, for example. The ERC-1155 standard is a more recent one. Tokens may be put into a single contract, giving you more options. Standardizing NFTS issuance improves interoperability. As a result, assets may be transported across platforms fast.

Choose a reliable wallet if you want to save money while still loving your NFTS. Your NFT will be delivered to the given address. NFTs cannot be replicated or transmitted without the permission of the owner.

On the OpenSea, NFT can be exchanged. They serve as a conduit between sellers and buyers, with each token having its own value. NFT prices change naturally as a result of market supply and demand.

But how useful is that? The worth of any valuable item is determined by those who value it. Mutual trust is the value. People have faith in fiat money, precious metals and automobiles.

Why isn't it saved digitally?

Every valuable object gains value in the same way. Money does not exist just to serve as a medium of transaction. People believe that money, whether it is fiat money, precious metals or vehicles, has value. Similarly, valuable goods gain value everywhere, which is why a digital library does not exist.

Where to Buy Digital Art

A lack of information and dissatisfaction, as well as precise questions and easily available solutions, are usually the best indicators that something is wrong.

Till recently, the majority of high-priced art was purchased through a gallery, a trade show or a marketplace, preferably after viewing it in its original state.

Observe how efficiently galleries and trade fairs are dismantling online viewing rooms as a step in the wrong direction, as a poor alternative for trade shows that will be hard to hold during the epidemic's start.

People are suddenly purchasing artwork on internet marketplaces that have no relation to the art world and, sometimes, do not even have a license to serve the conventional art audience.

Despite popular belief, even the largest and most popular markets, especially ones with constantly read auction records, depending on the internet artists and modern media artists' followers to make money. When you go through the drops on Nifty Gateway, for example, it's evident that the artists featured are explicitly picked based on the number of followers they have acquired.

Followers turn into collectors, and art is distributed in the same manner that shoes and hoodies are there are one-of-a-kind items and open groups. The bulk of the moment, artists publish one-of-a-kind items and open collections; this is how the high sales statistics are obtained.

The work can be purchased within a specific time frame, such as five minutes, seven minutes, or nine minutes; the number of sales determines the edition size. The cost of a single accessible collection normally ranges between $ 550 and $ 990. For $ 990, a limited edition of more than 100 pieces is sold. And all of this adds up.

Every day, new releases are released in the platform's newsletter on Nifty Gateway, the site launched by Griffin Cock Foster and Duncan. "TONIGHT'S drop will be accessible in 15 minutes!" it continues.

The server failed a few days ago during a dip due to a high volume of traffic. Of course, you could dismiss this as a brilliant marketing technique, bemoan the loss of quality, and argue that nothing is art. What does Christie plan to do with the Beeple NFT? Should those who made a fortune with Bitcoin and Ether invest in art and shop at Christie's?

In appearances and on Clubhouse, Kenny Schachter, the "Artnet" writer, dealer, gallerist, curator and artist, says it's all screensavers, gifts and video game stills when it comes to online art in the industry.

He characterized it as "like an object on the back of a car" in an appearance with "The Art Newspaper." Ne, like anything that originated on the Internet and is currently for sale on the Internet. And there are a plethora of memes, gifs, animations and renderings on the Internet that are relevant to the setting in which they were developed.

"Bad art is what people collect and adore," Lady Pheonix, an artist and a specialist at Clubhouse, explains. "Memes are going there," he adds.

What is the appearance of an NFT?

NFTs are impossible to touch since they may be anything digital - a painting, music, film, or even a cat GIF. Mike Winkelmann, akaBeeple, just sold his masterpiece Every Day: The First 5000 Days via Christie's for around $70 million.

He took a photo every day for 5000 days and has now compiled them into a single digital piece. The picture file and a non-fungible token are now delivered to the customer. The money has catapulted Winkelmann into the top three highest-paid living artists. And this is with a digital work of art that will never be able to be displayed on a wall.

When You See Yourself as NFT, the new album from Kings of Leon is out now. Six NFTs will be granted a golden ticket, ensuring them front-row seats for the rest of their life. Art activists purchased a Banksy photograph, digitized it, and then destroyed it. This picture is no longer available as an NFT and will be auctioned off on the OpenSea website.

OpenSea is the eBay of NFTs, and it's a huge success. In February, the site produced $86.3 million in sales, up from $8 million in January. Rarible and Nifty Gateway are two such auction websites.

If you want to get your hands on the Kings of Leon CD or one of the Golden Tickets, you'll need to delve deep into your digital wallet. NFTs are also being tested by FynnKliemann. He sold 100 jingles for 250,000 euros at auction.

People and organizations who can finance such tests are once again in the lead. Mark Cuban, a millionaire businessman, is one of them.

The NBA basketball league and FC Bayern Munich are also worth mentioning. So rare, a fantasy football platform may be thought of as a digital Panini album. The number of tickets available for individual footballers is quite restricted. The massive growth in worth.

So far, the most expensive trading card has been that of Paris Saint-Germain's Kylian Mbappé. It was sold for $57,000 dollars. The card cannot be counterfeited since it is recorded on the blockchain.

Coming to the Crypto Art

The current term in the media environment is "crypto art." On OpenSea, there's a lot of this "art." This digital work, including NFTs, can still be replicated, copied, and disseminated. You do not own the copyrights.

Only one aspect of NFTs cannot be copied: the authorship of the work. Artists retain complete ownership of the creation, just as they would with a traditional painting.

A Banksy poster may be purchased by anybody, but the original can only be possessed once.

Purpose of NFTs

For artists, it offers a chance to see money for their work, as well as the piece itself. Likes on Instagram are nice and all, but they don't pay you anything. In the event that the NFT is resold, the artist may get a part of the proceeds.

The jingles of Fynn Kliemann bring him 10 percent of every resale. As a purchaser, you see it as an opportunity to appreciate digital art in the same way that a museum does. In any scenario, it's a long-term business that should ultimately pay off.

There is also criticism of the hype.

NFTs wreak havoc on the environment. To clarify this, a small technical detour is required. The Ethereum blockchain, which serves as the base for NFTs, employs the Proof of Work mechanism.

Mining refers to the process of a computer solving complex puzzles in order to add new blocks to the blockchain. To prevent too much money from being earned too rapidly, the complexity of these jobs is artificially enhanced because of this, there is an arms race going on. Faster computers solve puzzles in less time, whereas new challenges slow computers down, necessitating greater processing power, which is then slowed down by more complex jobs.

It should go without saying that this concept is unlikely to win any sustainable prizes.

Are NFTs still worth it?

Of course, this assumes you have the necessary Cryptocurrencies. It's a business where supply and demand are the deciding factors. Crypto products, like conventional art, may be acquired and resold for a profit. Crypto products, like conventional art, may be acquired and resold for a profit. No one knows when the mentality will go down.

Crypto Hype: What Are NFTs Anyway?

Before we all go into NFT, let's define a blockchain and how non-fungible tokens fit into it. Bitcoin is, without a doubt, the most well-known blockchain initiative. The Bitcoin blockchain, on the other hand, can only be used to run a cryptocurrency network. This isn't true for every blockchain.

This is how data storage works in the blockchain.

In generally, a blockchain is a database made up of blocks that are connected together, just like links in a chain. Each block comprises the actual data to be kept in it on the one hand and a unique hash value on the other, ensuring that the data content remains intact.

In addition to its own hash value, every node in the network is aware of the prior block's hash value. In a chain reaction, the blockchain authenticates itself in this way. If any hash in the chain was modified, the chain would break.

As a result, data on the blockchain is more resistant to tampering than data in traditional databases. This feature is utilized by the so-called NFT.

Non-fungible tokens

The most common usage of the term token is as an asset. A token can also be used to represent an asset, an economic item or a digital representation of a physical commodity. All tokens in a cryptocurrency are fungible, that is, interchangeable.

This implies that each token is worth the same amount of money, regardless of which one you hold. It is worth the same as any other token possessed by a different bearer. This is also how our money operates. It makes no difference whether the ten-euro notes you use. You may also use any combination of two five-euro notes and five two-euro coins. The forms of payment, in this scenario, are interchangeable.

However, this is not the same case with NFT. Non-fungible tokens, or tokens that cannot be exchanged, represent a highly distinct asset and are thus one-of-a-kind. The only common thing among them and currency tokens are blockchain storage technology.

This makes NFT excellent for assets with only one or a few assets.

Digital trade cards, gaming characters, virtual expanses of land in virtual worlds, and so-called crypto art are presently examples. However, the blockchain might be used to store and protect identity cards, vaccination cards, and other essential papers.

Crypto collectibles and NFT art as dominant use cases currently.

At the moment, the most important or commonly utilized use cases of NFT are crypto art and digital collectibles. Let's start with the treasures.

Anyone who has played Magic the Gathering, Yu-Gi-Oh, or Pokémon with actual cards understands that having the appropriate cards is crucial to success.

There's also the urge to own extremely rare or popular cards, which is referred to as a collector's element, which caused the creation of a market where individual cards may be purchased for thousands of euros.

This model may be transferred to the blockchain via NFT. As a digital asset, a vehicle manufacturer might make 20 copies of a certain trading card and put them on the blockchain.

Now, 20 potential purchasers have the opportunity to purchase this item and afterward verify ownership.

Anyone who thinks this is just a theory might check out OpenSea, one of the largest of the now numerous NFT marketplaces. OpenSea is a virtual environment that features a variety of treasures and digital art pieces or assets that may be utilized in virtual worlds like Decentraland.

In early March 2021, BTC Echo announced the purchase of a digital area in the collecting monster game Axie Infinity for 1.5 million US dollars, or around 890 ethers, the Ethereum network's Cryptocurrency. The previous record-holder, the Cryptokitties Dragon, was overtaken by this transaction for what is perhaps the most well-known blockchain game, Cryptokitties. The cat, which has a dinosaur tail and looks like a hamster, was sold for 600 ether.

An increasing number of individuals are considering NFTs to offer digital creations that are guaranteed to be one-of-a-kind. With an NFT transaction on the Nifty Gateway platform, Canadian musician Grimes made roughly $6 million in less than 20 minutes. Fynn Kliemann, a German musician, is now auctioning 100 custom-made jingles as part of NFT. Leon's band Kings is selling their new album "When You See Yourself" on Open Sea in a 14-day bid.

Jack Dorsey, the CEO of Twitter, also wants in on the NFT craze. Just days before Twitter's 15th birthday, Dorsey is auctioning off an automated replica of the Valuables website's first tweet. The highest bid is presently $2.5 million.

Chapter 10. Future of Non Fungible Tokens

The popularity of NFT games has soared since its beginnings. Dapper Labs, the firm behind CryptoKitties, has been working with other NFT providers to improve interoperability amongst gaming platforms as of January 2019.

This implies that a native NFT from one platform may now be used on another without change. NFT initiatives have been developed by several large companies, like NBA and Ubisoft, which generate video games.

NFTs' potential has grown substantially in recent years, even beyond the gaming sector. A variety of companies are looking at nonfungible tokens to provide identity, certification, ticketing, and fractional possession of both virtual and analog assets.

NFT use cases cover any circumstance where there is a need for traceability and specific request.

The evolution of the Ethereum network and broader blockchain technology will significantly impact the future of NFTs.

NFTs will undoubtedly follow the development of blockchain systems, whether on the Ethereum blockchain, another public network or an internal network.

Crowdfunding is a non-fungible token

Nonfungible tokens are still a novel concept, and most game designers have had to find out how to make them on the fly. As a result, many NFTs are created utilizing pre-existing smart contracts or developing their protocol.

The NFT's inventors will also build a game to demonstrate the technology's capabilities and value in certain circumstances. This allows consumers to buy the game and give it a level of trustworthiness.

The NFT Approach to Crowdfunding

Crowdfunding to start a new business is a relatively new notion. Since 2015, NFTs (Non-Fungible Tokens) have been available on the Ethereum network. However, they are still relatively unknown among game producers and the general public.

As a result, many developers may lack the necessary tools or resources to design an NFT. One of the reasons for the NFT

Approach to Crowdfunding's inception was to overcome this problem. Using this technology, NFTs may now be built, hosted, and shared on any network (including mobile devices and web browsers).

Additionally, game makers can use the "NFT-Crowdfund" standard to create their crowdfunding campaign. It provides programmers with the techniques and support they need to develop their personal NFT.

This gives them the ability to generate their ERC-721 coin, a nonfungible token that may be used to support a crowdfunding campaign.

Creating NFT-Crowd fund

Here's how you can start your NFT-Crowdfunding campaign:

1) Using a platform (Ethereum Wallet, Metamask, etc.) or a command-line interface, create your colored token for crowdfunding (console).

2) Create and distribute NFTs using the NFT-Crowdfund protocol.

3) To describe your game components, use ERC 721.

4) Create discounted pre-order products using ERC – 684. After the Crowdfund expires, they will no longer be fungible. Unsold pre-order products are disposed of in a landfill.

5) Use the NFT registry to list your unique item(s) in a marketplace for post-crowdfunding sales or start your marketplace. If necessary, rename your NFT to match the name of the market. To check your new marketplace category, all pre-order products must be re-categorized.

1) Using a platform (Ethereum Wallet, Metamask, etc.) or a command-line interface, create your colored token for crowdfunding (console).

2) Create and distribute NFTs using the NFT-Crowdfund protocol.

3) To describe your game components, use ERC 721.

Hype Art NFT Marketplace

Finally, I'd like to introduce you to Hype Art, a groundbreaking endeavor. I'm working on a project with a group of art and cryptocurrency enthusiasts.

NFP (not-for-profit) ventures began to acquire traction. Even though bitcoin was experiencing a dip at the time, the sector grew significantly.

The most popular NFT marketplaces (Superrare, Niftigataway, Rarible) display their platforms in a style that resembles Amazon and eBay rather than an art gallery: collectors have no creative experience when perusing these platforms.

The artist is not the focal point of the conversation. The vision and thinking that went into its creation are given no consideration.

What do we want to create?

We believe that the NFT creator's artistic vision should be at the story's core. Each artist will be allowed to share the creative thought behind their work through a live interview (hosted by Koinsquare) and a selected summary of the work exhibited.

We want to establish a 3D virtual gallery that gives collectors the same experience as seeing artwork presented in a physical gallery.

We aim to use gamification to encourage the community of our collectors; thus, auctions will run concurrently with airdrops to our followers.

Where?

To get access to a larger market, Hype. Art will employ Opensea (ETH blockchain) and FAN (Tron blockchain) as auction platforms.

Instead, Hype. art will provide community-based creative marketing and an organized staff to allow artists to design their "online shows."

Conclusion

NFT is expected to be one of the most popular investment categories in 2022. Digital art is valuable in the eyes of the beholders, and NFTs make it possible to own a piece of this universe. Many questions remain unanswered in the world of new NFTs.

The inaugural tweet of Jack Dorsey was just sold for $2.5 million, paving the way for further similar transactions. Users have long desired monetization for the entire virtual world, and it is finally happening. Because the sale of in-game products has long been prohibited on auction sites such as eBay, the advent of NFTs provides gamers with a safer alternative to sell their efforts to others.

Hundreds of websites now claim to be able to provide authenticity certificates for everything from autographs to paintings in the physical world. As a result, even tangible artwork is traded via NFTs. By safeguarding everything on a single blockchain, it's now easier than ever to trade and authenticate these collectibles.

NFTs are a relatively new investment option. Some have been sold for tens of millions of dollars, demonstrating their viability. There is still a lot to learn regarding them. Furthermore, determining a fair price for digital art can be difficult, making NFTs a dangerous investment.

So, do you think NFTs are a good investment for you? The fundamentals of blockchain, bitcoin and NFTs are covered in this book, as well as how to value, create, buy, sell, trade, and invest in NFTs. If you choose to invest in NFTs, set a spending limit but only by how much you can afford to give up. As previously said, NFTs are highly speculative; thus, expecting to get wealthy right away is unrealistic. Additionally, keeping the majority of your money in safer products like ETFs and funds can be a good choice because you will be in a better position to take on riskier investments if the majority of your money is invested in relatively safe regions.

Because NFTs help collectors authenticate ownership, minimizing the risk of piracy and fraud, investors could expect higher prices for digital art classics. Also, don't be surprised if the value of physical collectibles rises.

At the same time, be wary of unanticipated dangers. It's possible that the value of Jack Dorsey's initial tweet may rise, but many more NFTs will fade away before the public realizes what they're worth.

NFTs are a fascinating new type of investment, but they aren't for everyone. It's not a terrible idea to have your feet wet if you're intrigued by NFTs and get some spare cash. Otherwise, it's better to wait on the sideline and watch the action develop from a safe distance, where your cash is safe.

Always exercise caution when making investments. It's an excellent moment to invest in NFTs, but don't risk more than you can afford to lose.

This book aims to inform readers on nonfungible tokens, including what they are and how they may help businesses. It delves into the specifics of the NFT market and where it is heading in the future. We also talk about the fallacies surrounding nonfungible tokens and what you can do to make your own.

This book should have given you a better knowledge of nonfungible tokens and how they could be used in your firm in the future.

www.ingramcontent.com/pod-product-compliance
Lightning Source LLC
Chambersburg PA
CBHW052326220526
45472CB00001B/288